"Whether you have just started to follow jesus or have been doing so for a number of years, Rodger Crooks' *The Good Book Guide* will provide you with a valuable resource for exploring the essentials of Christian belief."

(Roz Stirling – Presbyterian Church in Ireland Youth Officer)

"Interacting with a range of biblical texts and using contemporary language, Rodger Crooks is thought-provoking in his presentation of the main themes of the Christian faith."

(Dr Desi Alexander – Director of Christian Training, Presbyterian Church in Ireland)

"Rodger Crooks has written a timely, easy to read, freshly stimulating introduction to the Christian faith. It is an excellent resource for churches to use and for parents to give to their teenage children. I will certainly be doing so."

(Ian Hamilton – Cambridge Presbyterian Church, England)

"Healthy doctrine expressed in a fresh way. *The Good Book Guide* steers a course through deep waters with a deft touch. It is sure to be widely read."

(Dr Derek Thomas – Reformed Theological Seminary, Jackson, Mississippi)

"A rare gem among Reformed and Evangelical literature, attractively presented and illustrated, teaching solid truth in a contemporary style."

(Robert McCollum – Lisburn Reformed Presbyterian Church, Northern Ireland)

"Dr. Rodger Crooks has met a very real need here by providing a British based manual of our biblical and Presbyterian heritage suitable for all Christians but especially new ones."

(John Grier - Evangelical Bookshop, Belfast)

"*The Good Book Guide* is a good guide to the good Book! A helpful introduction to the Bible's teaching for young people, truth-seekers and new Christians."

(Alex J MacDonald – Buccleuch Free Church, Edinburgh)

© Rodger M Crooks
ISBN   1 85792 534 3

Published in 2001
by
Christian Focus Publications,
Geanies House, Fearn,
Ross-shire, IV20 1TW, United Kingdom.
www.christianfocus.com

Cover design by Alister MacInnes

THE GOOD BOOK GUIDE

EXPLORING THE BIBLE'S MAIN THEMES

Rodger M Crooks

Christian Focus

To the Belvoir Tabletalkers
– Rosie and Martyn,
Colin, Nichola, Denise, Michael and Christopher,
Jillian, Gary and Susan, Ross and Neil -
with the prayer that you might come to
"the knowledge of the truth that leads to godliness"
(Titus 1:1).

Also thanks to Gary Millar, Joy McKnight,
Beth Bogue, Noah Telling, Colin Millar, Desi Alexander
and Joan Crooks.
Your help, comments, patience
and encouragement were greatly appreciated.

CONTENTS

MEET *THE GOOD BOOK GUIDE*

The Good Book Guide, as its name suggests, is like a guidebook, trying to help you explore the main themes of the Bible. As you will soon discover, it is definitely not a novel, so you do not have to start with Chapter 1 and read right through to the end without skipping out any pages. Although I would encourage you to read each chapter in the order they appear in the book, there is absolutely nothing to stop you reading the chapters randomly, looking at whatever theme takes your fancy. I have just one word of advice to all you potential random readers – Chapters 11 and 12 will probably make more sense if you read Chapter 10 first.

Each chapter is made up of several components.

• At the start, there is a summary of the main points.

• There then follows the main teaching.

• Sprinkled liberally through the main teaching are boxed comments. These comments usually highlight how the chapter's teaching relates to everyday life. The point of this book is not just to give you more information about what the Bible says; I also want you to be a better Christian.

• At the end of each chapter I have suggested some books that will help you explore in greater detail the theme of that particular chapter. A word of warning – reading some of these books will make your brain hurt a little, but the rewards of getting to grips with what they say are well worth the effort.

1. THE STARTING POINT

> **In this chapter, we are going to discover what the Bible says about God.**
> **HE IS**
> - **Different from us**
>   - **Creator**
>   - **Sovereign**
>   - **Personal**
>   - **Father**
> - **Not just as Father, but also as Son and Holy Spirit**
> **HE IS NOT SILENT**
>   - **God speaks in creation**
>   - **God speaks in Jesus**
>   - **God speaks in the Bible**

In *The Sound of Music*, when Maria begins to teach the children to sing, she says, "Let's start at the very beginning. It's a very good place to start". Good advice for all wannabe singers, and for those wanting to explore the Christian faith. According to Maria, the starting point for anyone wanting to sing was "Doh, ray, me". What is the starting point for anyone trying to discover what Christians should believe? It is God. That is where the Bible begins. It opens with the majestic statement, "In the beginning, God…" (Genesis 1:1). So what is God like? We do not have to guess because the Bible informs us that God exists and speaks.

1. HE IS
The Bible never tries to prove God's existence. It assumes that everyone knows that God exists, and then goes on to tell us what He is like.

❖ DIFFERENT FROM US
The Bible emphasises that God is holy (Psalm 71:22, Psalm

99:3, 5 and 9, Isaiah 6:3 and Revelation 4:8), and when it does, the key idea is that He is different from us. Here are some ways in which God is totally different from us. God is eternal. Unlike us, He has no beginning or end. He has always existed and always will exist (Revelation 1:8). God is unchanging. Unlike us, He never grows old or tired (Isaiah 40:28), never changes His mind (Numbers 23:19) and never varies (Hebrews 13:8). His consistency means He is completely trustworthy and totally dependable. Unlike us, God needs no one else. As Father, Son and Holy Spirit, He is absolutely self-sufficient with no need for worshippers, helpers or defenders. God knows everything about everything and everybody all the time (Psalm 139:1-6). He does not have to access information, as a computer might retrieve a file, because all His knowledge is always in front of Him.

When people come face-to-face with God's holiness, they simply cannot cope (Isaiah 6:1-7; Luke 5:1-8 and Revelation 1:9-17). How do you react to this holy God? You could try to do the impossible and attempt to escape from Him. However, you will discover that you can run but you cannot hide (Psalm 139:7-12). Or you could do what John, Peter and Isaiah did - worship, follow and dedicate yourself to serve Him (Revelation 1:12-18, Luke 5:1-11 and Isaiah 6:1-8).

God's holiness is also seen in the aspects of His character, which we partially share with Him. God is loving, kind, merciful, wise, powerful, just, good and true, and because we are made in God's image, our lives are also characterised, to a limited degree, by these things. We must, however, realise that it is God's attributes, and not our experience of them, which determine our understanding of these things. If we let our own limited and finite experience determine our understanding of God's character, rather than His Word, we are guilty of idolatry, creating a man-made 'god' in place of the true and living God.

Jane grew up in an abusive household. She became a Christian at university, but due to her miserable relationship with her father, the idea of God's Fatherhood left her cold. "I thought God was like my father: merciless, demanding and unpredictable," she later admitted. "I allowed my life experiences to determine my view of God."

Jane turned away from her sin of projecting her experience-determined belief system onto God, and instead learnt to feed her mind with what the Bible said about God. Her life was transformed as she discovered that God is a merciful, faithful, consistent Father.

❖ **CREATOR**

In contrast to the idea of an impersonal and unplanned beginning to the universe, the Bible maintains that absolutely everything owes its existence to the creative activity of a wise, powerful and eternal God (Genesis 1:1). There were times, as in the creation of light, when He created out of nothing, using no pre-existing materials. He simply spoke and something that was not there before immediately existed (Genesis 1:3). At other times, as in the creation of Man, He used already existing materials and formed them into something else (Genesis 2:7). God created the universe, not because He was deficient and needed the creation to make up what was lacking in Him, but because it pleased Him to do so (Revelation 4:11) and in order to display His character (Psalm 19:1). The work of creation is usually assigned to God the Father. However, as in all other activities of God, God the Son and God the Holy Sprit were also involved in creation (Colossians 1:16 and Genesis 1:2).

The Bible also asserts that God is still active in His creation. Creation is not like a computer that has been left to run by itself. God actively sustains creation (Colossians 1:17 and Hebrews 1:3). If God withdrew from His creation, the universe would fall apart.

We might imagine that God has got so much on His plate in sustaining the universe, that He has little or no time for us. In Isaiah 40:27, that was the gripe the Israelites had with

God. "He's too busy to care for us," they moaned. God's response (Isaiah 40:28-31) is significant. The Israelites thought that God was too great to care for them. God's reply is that He is too great *not* to care for them. God's greatness is not seen in His aloofness; it is seen in His grace. He takes time to listen to us and to care for us by renewing us when we are drained, strengthening us when we feel weak and encouraging us when we despair. If God cares for sparrows, who are two a penny and not very important creatures, surely He will care for us, who are of supreme value to Him (Matthew 10:29 and 31).

❖ **SOVEREIGN**

A constant theme of the Bible is that God is king (Psalm 9:7, 10:16, 93:1, 96:10, 97:1, 99:1 and 146:10). The vision of God ruling from a throne is a recurring one. There are thirty-five references to God's throne in the book of Revelation alone. We must not imagine that God is a constitutional monarch with very limited powers. He is an absolute monarch with unrestricted powers. His sovereign rule is total: He does as He chooses (Isaiah 40:13-14) and no one can prevent Him from carrying out all He wills (Daniel 4:35).

The thought that God is sovereign is a massively stabilising factor in Christian living. God's ultimate purpose is to bring glory to Himself by saving us from sin and its horrible consequences, making us increasingly like Jesus, and bringing us safely home to heaven (Romans 8:29-30). Absolutely nothing or no one can stop Him from carrying out His purpose. He uses everything that happens to us, bad as well as good, to achieve the penultimate purpose of our spiritual well-being and the ultimate purpose of His glory (Romans 8:28).

❖ PERSONAL

Although we can say what He is like in terms of propositions, God is not a series of statements. He is a person - actually three persons. Like any other person, God wants us to know Him personally, and not just to know about Him. We must not fall into the trap of thinking that, because we know a great deal about God, we actually know Him. However, knowing God does depend on knowing about God. So, how do we turn our knowledge about God into knowledge of God? We make each truth we learn about God into a cause for thought and prayer before God, leading to obedience motivated by love for God.

> What effects does the knowledge of God have on people? J.I. Packer suggests that those who know God have great energy for God, have great thoughts of God, have great boldness for God, and have great contentment in God. Read Daniel 1-6 and 9, and trace out these themes in the lives of Daniel and his friends. Then ask yourself: how well do I know God?

❖ FATHER

Although it is found in the Old Testament, the idea of God as Father is seen most clearly in Jesus' teaching. The Bible emphatically states that God is the Father, not of everyone in general, but only of those who, knowing themselves to be sinners, have placed their trust in Jesus. Knowing God as Father is not a universal status that everyone has by being physically born, but a supernatural gift which people receive as a consequence of being spiritually re-born (John 1:12-13).

> The entire Christian life can be understood in terms of knowing God as Father.
> ➤ It is the basis of Christian conduct. Christian living is a matter of imitating the Father (Matthew 5:48 and Ephesians 5:1), glorifying the Father (Matthew 5:16 in King James Version, Romans 15:6 and 1 Peter 2:12) and pleasing

the Father (Romans 12:1-2 and Philippians 4:18).

➢ It is the basis of Christian prayer (Matthew 6:9). The Father is always accessible to His children. We can be bold and free in our prayers (Matthew 7:7-11). Like any wise father, God the Father reserves the right to say to His children, "No! That would not be good for you. Have this instead" (2 Corinthians 12:7-9).

➢ It is the basis of the life of faith (Matthew 6:25-27). If God cares for the birds, whose Father He is not, is it not obvious that He will care for us, whose Father He is? Instead of becoming anxious and getting into a flap, we are to trust our Father's wisdom and concentrate on living for Him (Matthew 6:25-33).

❖ NOT JUST AS FATHER, BUT ALSO AS SON AND HOLY SPIRIT

When we examine what the Bible says about God, we discover that, although there is only one God, He exists not only as Father but also as Son and Holy Spirit. Historically Christians have used the word "Trinity" to describe the complex relationship between God the Father, God the Son and God the Holy Spirit. Although the actual word is not found in the Bible, the idea definitely is and can be deduced from biblical data.

Although the Old Testament hints at the idea of the Trinity, its main emphasis is on the unity of God (Deuteronomy 6:4). However, the apostles, whose minds were saturated with the Old Testament conviction that God is one, came to see that Jesus was God the Son (Matthew 16:16) and that the Holy Spirit was also God (Acts 5:3-4). At the same time, they realised that the Father was not the Son or the Spirit, nor was the Son the Spirit.

When Christians tried to make sense of the biblical facts they had in front of them, namely that, within the one God, there are three distinct persons - the Father, the Son and the Holy Spirit - each of whom is said to be God, they realised that this information was not to be understood in terms of one god playing three different roles, or in terms of a belief in three gods. They put forward the idea of the Trinity as the only thing that does justice to all the biblical evidence. Question 6 of *The Shorter Catechism* summarises the Bible's teaching about the unity and triunity of God: "Three persons are in the one God - the Father, the Son and the Holy Spirit. These three are one God, the same in substance and equal in power and glory."

Cults, such as the Jehovah's Witnesses and Unitarians, reject the biblical idea of the Trinity. Do you know how to defend it? If you don't, read *Shared Life* by Donald Macleod (Published by Christian Focus Publications).

2. HE IS NOT SILENT

If we are to know what God is like in order to know Him personally, two barriers must be overcome. For a start, there is our ignorance of God. Left to our own devices, we do not have the mental ability to understand God's character (Isaiah 55:9). How can finite creatures possibly understand the infinite Creator? Then there is our sin before God. We do not want to have personal dealings with God because we do not want to give up our self-centred lifestyle (John 3:19-20). In His grace, God has broken down both these barriers. He has revealed Himself to us, so that we can know what He is like. He has also changed the basic orientation of our lives away from ourselves to Him, so that we long to know Him.

❖ GOD SPEAKS IN CREATION

God reveals Himself in a universal way through His creative activity (Psalm 19:1). Writing in Romans 1:18-24, Paul points out that, as a result of His general revelation in creation, everyone not only knows that God exists, but they also know something about God. They know that God is their Creator, who demands that they worship and obey Him, and will, one day, as their Judge, require them to give an account to Him of how they have lived.

However, because they want to think and live independently of God, people stifle this limited knowledge of God, and worship substitutes for God. Their action is inexcusable.

> Romans 1:19-20 highlights the great problem faced by those who claim to be atheists or agnostics. In spite of what they say, they know in their hearts that there is a God. No human being, regardless of race, personality, class, gender or religious background, will be able to stand before God and claim, "I never knew You existed. If only You had revealed Yourself I would have believed". There will be no acceptable excuses on Judgment Day. The reason why people claim to be atheists or agnostics is because they want to think independently of God in order to live in rebellion against Him (Romans 1:18 and 20-32).
> We do need to try and answer their intellectual problems. However, when speaking to such people about the gospel, it is essential that we realise that it is their moral revolt against God that gives rise to their intellectual problems. This can be seen in Jesus' conversation with the Samaritan woman beside the well at Sychar (John 4:1-26).

❖ GOD SPEAKS IN JESUS

God's revelation in creation not only has a general audience, but also has a general content. It does not reveal all that we need to know about God in order to be saved. This kind of revelation only occurred when God Himself, in the person of Jesus His Son, came to earth and spoke to us (John 1:14 and 18). In Jesus' character and actions we see what God's character is like (Colossians 1:15 and Hebrews 1:3). Jesus could say that anyone who knows what He is like, knows what God is like (John 14:9).

> Just as human beings disclose their character in their actions, so God showed Himself to us in Jesus' death. In fact, Jesus' death is the clearest revelation of God's

character. The cross tells us that God is love (1 John 4:9-10), just (Romans 3:25), wise (1 Corinthians 1:18-24), and powerful (1 Corinthians 1:18-24).

❖ GOD SPEAKS IN THE BIBLE

The Bible claims to be God's Word in which He speaks to us today (2 Timothy 3:16). There is no conflict between God speaking to us in Jesus and God speaking to us in the Bible. The Bible contains the Old Testament, which Jesus personally endorsed as pointing forward to Him (John 5:39). The Bible contains the New Testament gospels, which give us the authoritative record of Jesus' teaching and actions (Mark 1:1). The Bible contains the New Testament letters, which Jesus authorised His apostles to write and promised them the Holy Spirit to help them with this process (John 14:26 and 16:13). As we read the Bible, the written Word, through the activity of the Holy Spirit, we hear the voice of Jesus, the living Word.

Several terms are used in connection with the Bible.

➤ The Bible is *inspired*. Although human authors wrote it, the Bible ultimately came from God and so can be called God's Word (2 Timothy 3:16 and 2 Peter 1:20-21).

➤ The Bible is *infallible*. The Bible is true because it comes from a God who cannot lie (Numbers 23:19), has as its focus Jesus who claimed to be the Truth (John 14:6), and is inspired by the Spirit of truth (John 16:13). It is the only reliable guide to how we can honour God and experience His blessing in our lives. "The only authority for glorifying and enjoying [God] is the Bible, the Word of God, which is made up of the Old and New Testaments" (*The Shorter Catechism* Question 2).

➤ The Bible is *authoritative*. It is to control our thinking and behaviour as it teaches, rebukes, corrects and trains us in right living (2 Timothy 3:16). Submitting to Jesus'

18

lordship means doing what the Bible says (Luke 6:46 and John 13:13 and 17). Being filled and controlled by the Spirit is the same as obeying the Bible (Compare Ephesians 5:18-20 with Colossians 3:16-17).

➢ The Bible is *sufficient*. The Bible does not give us the answer to every single question ever asked. In His wisdom, God has decided to keep some of His counsel to Himself. However, what He does want us to know He has revealed in the Bible, and it contains everything we need so that we can live for Jesus (Deuteronomy 29:29 and 2 Peter 1:3).

The Bible is *complete*. God no longer speaks directly to people as He once did. God has said all that He has to say in Jesus, His final Word (Hebrews 1:1-2). He has nothing more to add. There are no supplements to the Bible.

In 1543 Nicolaus Copernicus turned the astronomical world of his day on its head when he published a book called *Concerning the Revolution of the Celestial Spheres*. Up to that point people had believed that the earth was the centre of the universe. Copernicus suggested that it was not. His theory laid the foundation for the planetary laws of Johannes Kepler, who showed that the sun, not the earth, was the centre of our solar system.

Self-centred me-ism is the controlling philosophy of most people's lives today. People think that the universe revolves around them. They believe that, if God exists, He exists to help and serve them. We need a Copernican style revolution in our thinking about God. We need to urgently realise that *He* is the centre of the universe, not us, grasping that it is "in Him that we live and move and have our being" (Acts 17:28). We were made to worship and glorify Him, not the other way round. However, we must also grasp that when we do love Him with all of our being (Matthew 22:37-38), we will experience life in all its richness and fullness (John 17:3).

DIGGING DEEPER

You might like to explore further some of the issues raised in this chapter by reading *Knowing God* by J.I. Packer (Published by Hodder), *A Heart for God* by Sinclair Ferguson (Published by Banner of Truth) and *Discovering God* by Philip G Ryken (Published by IVP).

2. THE GREAT ENIGMA

> **In this chapter, we are going to discover what the Bible says about human beings.**
> **HUMAN DIGNITY**
> - **Human beings are the high point of God's creation**
> - **Human beings are unique in God's creation**
> - **Human beings are made in God's image**
> **Dominion, worship, intelligence, responsibility and community**
> **HUMAN DISGRACE**
> - **At its most fundamental, sin is blasphemous rebellion against God**
> - **Sin has vandalised God's image in us**
> - **Sin has affected everyone**
> - **Sin has polluted every part of our personality**

In *Prince Caspian*, one of C.S. Lewis' Narnia stories, the children, Peter, Susan, Edmund and Lucy are suddenly pulled back into Narnia to help Prince Caspian rescue its inhabitants from evil. When Aslan the Lion meets them, he makes this remark: "You are from the Lord Adam and the Lady Eve. And that is both honour enough to erect the head of the poorest beggar, and shame enough to bow the shoulders of the greatest emperor on earth." That statement captures the great enigma human beings are - special, but, at the same time, sinful.

1. HUMAN DIGNITY
Human dignity has its roots in the fact that God created us.

❖ HUMAN BEINGS ARE THE HIGH POINT OF GOD'S CREATION
God did not create the universe in an instant. He did so in stages, with each stage building upon the previous one. The last of God's creative acts, carried out at the end of the sixth day of

creation, was to make human beings.

In Genesis 1, each stage of creation is introduced by a command – "And God said, 'Let…'" (Genesis 1:3, 6, 9, 14, 20 and 24). Humanity's creation, however, is introduced by a conversation. God pauses and deliberates with Himself (Genesis 1:26) before creating human beings (Genesis 1:27). Although humans were made from already existing materials (Genesis 2:7), the conversation God had with Himself indicates that they were going to be brilliantly new. With the creation of human beings, God's creative activity was going to reach its climax.

In Genesis 1, the verb "to create" is used three times (Genesis 1:1, 21 and 27). First when God created matter from nothing; then when He created conscious life; and finally when He created humanity. This progression points to humans as being the apex of creation.

After God had created humanity, He was finished. He announced that He was delighted with His creation (Genesis 1:31). As nothing more needed to be created, God rested (Genesis 2:1-3).

❖ HUMAN BEINGS ARE UNIQUE IN GOD'S CREATION

Humans are special in creation. Although we are part of creation, we are set apart from creation. Genesis 2:7 describes humanity's creation. The Bible does not allow the idea that we are simply the result of the mutation of the gene of some other animal. Between humans and other forms of creation there is such a gap that only God's creative activity can bridge it. With loving care, God formed Adam, the first human being, culminating in God breathing "into his nostrils the breath of life" (Genesis 2:7). The very first breath a human breathes is his Maker's. When he opens his eyes for the very first time, Adam is looking into his Maker's face. This did not happen to any other of creature. We did not simply evolve; God uniquely formed us.

Although they are unique in creation, humans also have a close correspondence with the rest of the organic creation. The Bible teaches this by reminding us that God made humans from dust, already existing material, and by not allocating a separate day of creation to human beings. Saying there is an anatomical correspondence between a human being and an ape, and a physiological correspondence between a human and a pig does not violate the Bible's teaching. Nor does this correspondence require the conclusion that humans are simply a development of these other animals. The correspondence is not due to evolution, but to the fact of a common Creator duplicating His systems in more than one form of His creation.

Only human beings are made in God's image (Genesis 1:26). There is nothing higher than humanity in all creation because humans alone carry God's image.

Although we are the high point of creation and unique in creation, human beings are still creatures. This is seen in the fact that we cannot live in independence of God.

➢ Human beings are dependent on God for physical life (Genesis 2:7 and Acts 17:28). We cannot move a muscle, think a thought or feel an emotion unless God gives us the ability to do so.

➢ Human beings are dependent on God for companionship (Genesis 2:18-25). It was God who made the woman and brought her to the man so that together they might complement and provide friendship and love for each other. In doing so, God established life-long heterosexual marriage as the norm for society. Anything that deviates from this norm is a distortion of God's good design for His creation.

➢ Human beings are dependent on God for guidance (Genesis 2:16). Right from the beginning, human beings were not able to work out for themselves what was right and what was wrong. They needed God to tell them.

Only God is self-sufficient. Humans, on the other hand, need God.

❖ HUMAN BEINGS ARE MADE IN GOD'S IMAGE

Humans, who are made in the image of God, resemble Him.

Dominion (Genesis 1:26 and 28) Because we share God's image, we share God's rule. We act in God's place, controlling the rest of creation for God's glory and our benefit. This involves domesticating the animals and putting them to work, carrying out scientific research and development, harnessing the earth's resources and cultivating the land.

In a society where to be green does not mean to be naïve, how should a Christian view the environment?

➤ We are to be thankful for the world God made and praise Him for it (1 Timothy 4:4). The idea that matter is evil must be rejected. Instead we value everything because God made everything.

➤ We should delight in creation. The magnificence of a sunset, the grandeur of the mountains, the crispness of a frosty morning, the dampness of a rain forest, the crunch of snow, the fragrance of a rose garden and the melody of the dawn chorus are all gifts from God for us to enjoy.

When we become Christians everything is new (2 Corinthians 5:17). Our emotions and senses are now sharper and more sensitive than before we were converted. Therefore, Christians should appreciate creation more than unbelievers.

➤ We should demonstrate a responsibility towards the environment. We must work with God's creation, giving thought to the value and purpose of everything in creation.

Creativity Having been created in a Creator's image, human beings have the ability to be creative too. So we draw and paint, write prose and poetry, compose and play music, and design and build. Through our senses we can appreciate what is beautiful, lovely, noble, excellent and admirable.

Worship Humans alone have an in-built capacity to enter

into a personal relationship with God. We must worship; it is part of what it means to be human. We worship the true and living God, or we worship self-designed substitute gods. Either way, in Bob Dylan's words, we've "gotta serve somebody".

Intelligence Genesis 1 portrays God as a thinker and planner, who worked out everything before He did it, and as an assessor, who was able to evaluate everything He did. Humans, as God's image-bearers, can think and reason. We have the ability to stand outside of ourselves and to be self-critical. We have a ravenous hunger to know more, so we are constantly trying to push out the boundaries of knowledge further and further.

Responsibility God treats us as responsible moral beings. He issued commands to Adam and Eve (Genesis 2:16-17) and expected them, out of love for Him, to deliberately choose to obey His instructions. When Adam and Eve did not do this and tried to blame each other for their disobedience (Genesis 3:12-13), God refused to let them shift the blame unto someone else. He made them carry the can for their actions (Genesis 3:16-17), and God's punishment of Adam and Eve (Genesis 3:23-24) shows that He treated them as moral beings who were responsible for their actions. The idea of right and wrong is meaningless to an animal. Animals can be trained to do certain things and not to do others, but they cannot be taught that some things are right while others are wrong. Yet right and wrong are terms we understand. So we feel good when we do what we think is right, and we feel guilty and shabby when we do what we perceive is wrong.

Community God lives in community (Genesis 1:26), so we too like to enjoy relationships with other human beings. We like to be with other people, taking pleasure from their company and friendship. If, for any reason, we find ourselves cut off from others, we get lonely and out of sorts.

In our society dehumanising forces are at work, undermining our dignity as creatures made in God's image.

26

> In the blame culture that exists today, someone is to blame for everything that happens - except us, of course! Even if we are in the wrong, we are told never to admit to anything. When he was challenged about something he did, Bart Simpson replied, "I didn't do it. Nobody saw me do it. You can't prove anything." We are conditioned not to hold up our hand and say that it was our fault. This subverts the idea of human responsibility.

> The cult of the individual, which tells us that we do not need other people and that we can manage by ourselves, destabilises the idea of community.

> Materialism is rampant in our society. People are seduced into thinking that all reality is only what we can experience with our senses. Materialism robs us of the idea that we have a God-orientation in our lives, being made to know, worship and serve Him.

Can you think of any other dehumanising forces at work in our society?

Human dignity is supremely seen in Jesus, who became a real human being. If we want to see what it means to be human, we need to look at Jesus' life. God also gloriously endorsed human dignity in Jesus' coming to earth. When God acted in salvation, He did not become an angel or an animal; He became a human.

If this was all the Bible said about human beings, it would be a totally misleading picture of human nature. It is true that human beings were created sinless, but we know from many sources, not least our own experience, that this is not the way things are now. Somewhere we went horribly wrong. In Genesis 3, in an event known as "The Fall", the Bible describes how humanity fell from this original condition of innocence and purity.

2. HUMAN DISGRACE

What the Bible says about this dark side to our humanity is not pretty. When human beings, who were made by God for God, turned away from God, it was the biggest catastrophe ever to happen because after The Fall the whole of humanity nose-dived into sin.

❖ **AT ITS MOST FUNDAMENTAL, SIN IS BLASPHEMOUS REBELLION AGAINST GOD**

Human beings fell from their original condition of sinless dignity because Adam and Eve helped themselves to fruit from the Tree of the Knowledge of Good and Evil (Genesis 3:1-11). The question of what kind of fruit it was is totally irrelevant. The important issue is what the fruit symbolised. God had told Adam and Eve that they could eat from any tree in the Garden of Eden, except for one - the Tree of the Knowledge of Good and Evil (Genesis 2:16-17). The fruit of that tree symbolised that they were creatures under God's authority. It reminded them that they were not God, but were responsible to Him.

God's instructions to Adam and Eve could not have been clearer. They knew that they could look but they better not touch. So, when Adam and Eve ate the fruit, they were deliberately rebelling against God. They were saying to God, "You are not going to tell us what to do. We are going to do what we want to do". In their bid for independence, they were setting themselves up as 'God'. They were going to play at being God, deciding what was right and wrong for them (Genesis 3:5), rather than letting God tell them what was right and wrong.

Jesus' death confirms that, at its most fundamental, sin is blasphemous rebellion against God. In His death, Jesus was dying in our place, being punished for our sins. He was executed for two crimes - the crime of blasphemy, claiming to be God (Mark 14:61-64) and the crime of rebellion (Mark 15:26). The charges levelled against Jesus signal what the essence of sin is.

The Bible uses a variety of words to describe sin.

> ➤ Sin is crookedness. The Bible word is "unrighteousness" (Romans 1:18 in the King James Version). Righteousness carries with it the idea of straightness and conforming to God's standards as set out in His Law. Sin is deliberately doing what we know to be out of line with God's norm.
>
> ➤ Sin is failure (Romans 3:23). In the penalty shootout between England and Argentina to settle one of the quarter-finals of the 1998 soccer World Cup, David Batty missed. His failure from the penalty spot sent England crashing out of the competition. Sin is our failure to do what God tells us to do. Most people think that sin is only doing wrong. However, the majority of sins fall into this category of failure.
>
> ➤ Sin is self-centredness. The Bible word is "iniquity" (Psalm 51:2). We are twisted, turned in on ourselves.
>
> ➤ Sin is repudiating God and His instructions. The Bible word is "lawlessness" (1 John 3:4). We do not just defy God's Law; we reject it out of hand. We throw off God's instructions, and go our own way (Isaiah 53:6). We claim that there are no absolutes to live by, but we do live by an absolute - our own desires. We are a law unto ourselves.
>
> ➤ Sin is straying off the right path. The Bible word is "trespass" (Romans 5:15). In the Bible, God has shown us the way to live (Psalm 119:105), but we have strayed from it, preferring our own ideas to God's (Jeremiah 18:12).

❖ **SIN HAS VANDALISED GOD'S IMAGE IN US**

Human beings never cease to bear God's image. However, as a result of the Fall, it has been spoiled and distorted almost beyond recognition. Human beings still worship, but we worship substitute gods. Rather than loving God, we love money, pleasure and ourselves (2 Timothy 3:1-4). Human beings still have the capacity to think, but we either do not think or our thinking is twisted. Contemporary society is largely anti-intellectual, and has become almost exclusively feeling-orientated. We do not ask people, "What do you think about this?" Instead we ask them, "How do you feel about this?" The old philosophical maxim "I think therefore I am" has been replaced by "I feel therefore I am". Even when we do think, we have the twisted capacity to turn things on their head, calling right wrong and wrong right.

Human beings are still responsible, but we often act irresponsibly. We seldom think about the consequences of our actions. We are so selfish that we do what is wrong even though we know it will hurt others. We are so short-termist that we indulge in harmful practices even though we know that in the long run our habits will damage us. Human beings must still live together, but we drive wedges between others and ourselves. Our critical attitudes, gossiping tongues, snobbery, unforgiving spirit and pride create barriers to friendships and a sense of community. Human beings still have an obligation to manage the earth sensibly, but we misuse our dominion. We pollute the planet and squander its resources. Human beings have turned the reason why God gave us creative abilities on its head, using them to draw attention to human achievements, to express our rebellion against God and to seduce others away from the truth.

> **The aim of God's activity in our lives is to restore the beauty of His image in us (Romans 8:29).**

❖ SIN HAS AFFECTED EVERYONE

In the opening section of his letter to the Christians in Rome, Paul analyses the lifestyles of irreligious people (Romans 1:18-32), decent, moral people who do not claim to be religious (Romans 2:1-16), and religious people (Romans 2:17-3:8). His summary makes disturbing reading. He concludes that everyone has sinned. Sin is a universal disease, from which none of us is immune. Our own experience backs up Paul's conclusion. Although we have to be taught many things in life, we do not have to be taught to sin;

it comes naturally to us.

The universal problem of sin stems from the fact that, when Adam sinned, he was not acting solely on his own behalf, but the Bible states that he was acting as the representative of all humanity (Romans 5:12-17). Just as a national leader involves the people he represents in the consequences of his action when, for instance, he declares war, so Adam involved the people he represented, namely all his descendants, in the consequences of his sin. When Adam sinned, we sinned as well. Just as children inherit their parents' characteristics, so everyone ever born inherits from Adam his blasphemous, rebellious mindset. We do not become sinners because we sin. We were born sinful, and we sin because we are sinners. The Bible declares, "there is no one righteous", and then hammers the final nail into the coffin of any idea that we are basically good by adding "not even one" (Romans 3:10).

❖ SIN HAS POLLUTED EVERY PART OF OUR PERSONALITY

No aspect of our personality has escaped the ravages of sin. The Bible draws our attention to the fact that sin has polluted our minds (Romans 3:11). People are in the dark about God's ways. After they have had the way of salvation explained simply and clearly to them, they still scratch their heads and say to themselves, "What on earth was he talking about?"

Sin has polluted our emotions (Romans 3:18). People are not terrified by the thought of their blasphemous rebellion against God. They could not care less. It's no big deal. Sin causes us to misdirect our ability to love. Instead of loving God and our neighbour, we love ourselves. Sin has also polluted our wills (Romans 3:12). We cannot do what is good, namely trusting in and serving God.

It is essential that we distinguish between free will and human responsibility. The Bible teaches that God treats us as being fully responsible for all our actions. We do not sin by accident but because we choose to do so. Even when we are sinned against, God expects us not to sin in response. If we do sin, God holds us responsible. However, the idea of human responsibility does not mean that our wills are free. Ever since the Fall our wills have been controlled by sin. They are not free; instead they are in bondage. The Bible teaches that we are morally responsible beings, yet at the same time, we are slaves to sin until Jesus comes, by His Spirit's activity, to change our wills and to take control of them. A great deal of sterile controversy over the freedom of our wills would be avoided if we learnt to distinguish between free will and human responsibility.

In Romans 3:13-17, Paul lists different parts of our bodies - our throats, tongues, lips, mouths, feet and eyes. These limbs and organs were given to us so that through them we might glorify God and serve others. Instead, we use them to harm people and to rebel against God. This is what is known as "Total Depravity". It is not that everyone is as bad as they could possibly be, but that sin has polluted, twisted and stained every part of our humanity.

Even when we become Christians, we are still not free from the devastating effects of sin. Although the basic orientation of our lives has been radically altered, Christians still sin. Before we became Christians, we developed sinful habits as we responded sinfully to the various situations in which we found ourselves. We carry these sinful habits into our Christian lives. God's activity in making us more like Jesus - an activity known as "sanctification" - is not simply a matter of breaking these sinful habits, but also of replacing them with alternative biblical habits.

➢ Our lives are transformed to become increasingly like Jesus as we learn, not only to stop doing and saying what is wrong, but also by starting to do and say what is right. In

Ephesians 4:22 and 24 and Colossians 3:5, Paul explains that sanctification involves putting off sinful patterns of speech and behaviour and then putting on biblical patterns of speech and behaviour in their place, just as we would take off dirty smelly clothes and put on fresh clean clothes.

➤ Our lives are transformed to become increasingly like Jesus as we learn to be what we are. God has changed us radically, so we are to show this change in the way we live (Ephesians 5:8, Colossians 3:12).

This is the great enigma of our humanness: our dignity and our disgrace. One minute we behave like God, in whose image we were made, and the next we act like animals, from whom we were meant to be distinct. Like the Jekyll and Hyde creatures we are, we have set up hospitals for the care of the sick, but we have also set up concentration camps. Our need is for a salvation that both cleanses us from sin's pollution and gives us new hearts with new perspectives, ambitions and desires. The good news of the Christian message is that God offers us such a salvation. In the person of Jesus, He came after us and died our death so that we might be forgiven. Then He sent His Holy Spirit to change our personalities from within, so that His Son's likeness might be renewed in us.

DIGGING DEEPER

You might like to explore further some of the issues raised in this chapter by reading *Being Human: The nature of spiritual experience* by Ronald Macauley and Jerram Barrs (Published by Solway) and *The Christian View of Man* by J. Gresham Machen (Published by Banner of Truth).

3. THE HEART OF THE MATTER

In this chapter, we are going to discover what the Bible says about Jesus' claim to be God.

JESUS MADE UPFRONT CLAIMS TO BE GOD
- Jesus' description of Himself
- Jesus' "I am" statements
- Jesus' close identification with God
- The pretext for executing Jesus

JESUS MADE INDIRECT CLAIMS TO BE GOD
- Jesus claimed that He could forgive sins
- Jesus claimed that He could give life
- Jesus claimed that He would judge the world

JESUS' MIRACLES WERE POINTERS TO HIS DEITY

JESUS' SINLESSNESS REINFORCED HIS CLAIM TO BE GOD
- What Jesus thought of Himself
- What Jesus' friends thought of Him
- What Jesus' enemies thought of Him

Bob looked across the table at me and said, "Do you not think that you Christians put all your eggs in one basket?" "What do you mean?" I replied. "Well," he answered, "everything about Christianity seems to revolve around Jesus". Bob had hit the nail on the head. Who Jesus is lies at the heart of the Bible's message.

The Shorter Catechism gives a brilliant summary of the Bible's teaching about who Jesus is. It states that "the Lord Jesus Christ [is] the eternal Son of God, who became Man. He was and continues to be God and Man in two distinct natures and one person forever" (Question 21). Jesus is 100% God and at the same time 100% human. He is the God-Man (1 Timothy 2:5). In this chapter we are going to explore the fact that He is fully God, and then, in the next chapter, we will tease out the reality of His full humanity.

> The New Testament writers unashamedly put Jesus forward as being 100% God.
>
> ➤ John states that "the Word was God" (John 1:1), and then he goes on to identify Jesus as the Word (John 1:14).
>
> ➤ The writer of Hebrews asserts that "the Son is the radiance of God's glory" (Hebrews 1:3), so that just as sunlight reflects the sun's glory, so Jesus reflects God's glory because He is God the Son.
>
> ➤ In Colossians 2:9, Paul claims that "in Christ, all the fullness of the Deity lives in bodily form." The Greek word for "fullness" implies that Jesus is maximum capacity God. He could not be any more God than He was.

Critics of biblical Christianity claim that, although the New Testament writers did believe that Jesus was God, it was only because they read that idea back into Jesus' life, and that Jesus Himself never claimed to be God. However, on examining the evidence, we can see that the conclusion of these critics. is out of 'sync' with the data.

1. JESUS MADE UPFRONT CLAIMS TO BE GOD

Matthew, Mark, Luke and John, the writers of the Gospels, record several ways in which Jesus directly claimed to be God.

❖ JESUS' DESCRIPTION OF HIMSELF

Jesus' preferred self-designation was the title "the Son of Man". Rather than being a contrast to the title "the Son of God" and so pointing to His humanity, "the Son of Man" actually alludes to Jesus' deity. The title has its roots in Daniel 7:13-14, in which Daniel relates part of a dream he had. In it he saw a figure that he describes as being "like a son of man". Daniel's Son of Man is a divine figure. Although he was human in that he was *like* a son of man, he was more than that; He was superhuman. He was royal in that he was given universal and eternal authority. He was divine in that he came "with the clouds of heaven" - a symbol of God's presence in the Old Testament (Exodus 24:16, Numbers 9:16 and 1 Kings 8:10). Jesus picks up this motif of a majestic, divine Son of Man, and applies it to Himself. So, when Jesus describes Himself as "the Son of Man", He is making an explicit claim to be God.

❖ JESUS' "I AM" STATEMENTS

Seventeen times in John's Gospel, Jesus uses the phrase "I am" when He refers to Himself. Those two seemingly innocent words often got Him into hot water with the Jewish religious establishment. One example is recorded in John 8:56-58. Jesus is challenged about His statement that Abraham had seen Him and was ecstatically glad. They thought Jesus was crazy. "You are not even fifty!" they jeered. "How could you have seen Abraham?" Jesus replied, "Before Abraham was, I am!" Something in that statement caused the Jewish religious leaders to see red, because they immediately picked up rocks and tried to stone Jesus to death. What provoked such a violent reaction? It was not Jesus' bad grammar. It was the fact that Jesus described Himself as "I am", which was God's special name (Exodus 3:13-14). The Jewish religious leaders knew what Jesus was driving at. He was claiming to be God.

John records seven special statements that Jesus made all beginning with the phrase "I am." - "I am the Bread of Life" (John 6:35), "I am the Light of the world" (John 8:12), "I am the Door" (John 10:7 and 9), "I am the Good Shepherd" (John 10:11 and 14), "I am the Resurrection and the Life" (John 11:25), "I am the Way, the Truth and the Life" (John 14:6) and "I am the true Vine" (John 15:1 and 5).

What is striking about these seven statements is how self-focused they are. In these "I am" statements Jesus is claiming that He alone is everything human beings need to enjoy a full spiritual life. Only someone who believed that

He was God would make such a staggering claim.

❖ Jesus' close identification with God

Jesus identified Himself so closely with God that He claimed our attitude to Him was the same as our attitude to God. To know Jesus is to know God (John 8:19 and John 14:7). To see Jesus is to see God (John 14:9). To believe in Jesus is to believe in God (John 12:44 and John 14:1). To welcome Jesus is to welcome God (Mark 9:37). To hate Jesus is to hate God (John 15:23). To honour Jesus is to honour God (John 5:23).

Some try to side-step Jesus' claim to be God by saying He is a great religious teacher, suggesting He is on a par with Mohammed, the Buddha and the other great teachers of the world's religions. Some would even go as far as saying that Jesus was the best of the lot. The problem with saying that about Jesus is that He never claimed to be merely top of the class. He claimed that He was in a class of His own. Jesus claimed that, in comparison to Him, all other religious teachers were not really at the game. They were merely human, while He was God. C.S. Lewis, in his book *Mere Christianity*, puts to bed this idea that Jesus was just a great religious teacher. "A man who was merely a man and said the sort of things Jesus said would not be a great teacher. He would either be a lunatic - on the level with the man who says he is a poached egg - or else He would be the devil of hell. You must make your choice. Either this man was, and is, the Son of God: or else a madman or something worse. You can shut Him up for a fool, you can spit at Him and kill Him as a demon; or you can fall at His feet and call Him Lord and God. But let us not come to any patronising nonsense about Him being a great human teacher. He has not left that open to us. He did not intend to."

❖ **THE PRETEXT FOR EXECUTING JESUS.**

The Jewish religious establishment finally arrested Jesus and put Him on trial before the Sanhedrin, their religious court. Plenty of people were willing to bring trumped up charges against Him, but their evidence did not add up. In his desperation to have some pretext on which he could have Jesus put to death, the Chief Priest asked Him point blank if He was God. Even though He knew it would lead to His certain execution on the charge of blasphemy, Jesus replied that He was (Mark 14:61-64).

Matthew, Mark, Luke and John's data show Jesus Himself explicitly coming out as God.

2. JESUS MADE INDIRECT CLAIMS TO BE GOD

Jesus set out His stall to be God as forcefully by indirect means as by direct means. The things Jesus did signalled that He was God as much as His open claims about Himself. On several occasions, Jesus carried out activities that people normally associate with God.

❖ **JESUS CLAIMED HE COULD FORGIVE SINS**

I overheard two ladies gossiping in the supermarket. One said to the other, "God forgive me for saying this, but…" and then proceeded to run down one of their neighbours! Forgiving sins is something associated with God, and Jesus did it. He forgave an immoral woman, who had gatecrashed a dinner party to which He had been invited (Luke 7:36-50). He also forgave a paraplegic, whose friends had lowered him down through the roof of the house in which He was teaching (Mark 2:1-12).

When He forgave and healed the paraplegic, Jesus asked His critics this question: "Which is easier: to say, 'Your sins are forgiven,' or to say, 'Get up, take your mat and walk'?" (Mark 2:9). What is the answer to Jesus' question? It was easier to say, "Your sins are forgiven" because forgiveness is something that takes place internally so there was no

38

observable way of proving that he had been forgiven. It was much harder to say, "Get up, take your mat and walk" because people would see if the paraplegic did roll up his mat and walk home. To show that He could do something that people could not see, namely forgive sins, Jesus did something that people could see, namely heal the paraplegic.

❖ **JESUS CLAIMED HE COULD GIVE LIFE**

Again giving life is something that people associate with God. Jesus claimed that He could give life. In fact, Jesus said that one of the reasons why He came into the world was to give people spiritual life (John 10:10) and that experiencing spiritual life was inextricably linked to trusting in Him (John 3:16 and 36).

❖ **JESUS' CLAIMED HE WOULD JUDGE THE WORLD**

Judging the world is another activity linked to God. Not only did Jesus say that He would judge the world (John 5:27), but that His criterion of judgment would be people's attitude to Him as demonstrated by their response to His teaching (John 12:47-48).

3. JESUS' MIRACLES WERE POINTERS TO HIS DEITY

A recent animated film about Jesus' life is called *The Miracle Maker*. Although He was more than a miracle worker, Jesus did perform miracles. Why? In order to back up His claim to be God. Jesus' miracles were signposts, pointing to His deity.

The word that John prefers to use when he describes Jesus' miracles is the word "sign". Jesus' miracles were not naked displays of power designed to impress the masses. Jesus' miracles were signs that "revealed His glory" (John 2:11). In other words, they tell us who Jesus is. In his Gospel, John highlights seven miracles Jesus performed - Jesus turned water into wine (John 2:1-11), healed a civil servant's sick son (John 4:43-54), cured a paralysed man

39

who was lying beside the Pool of Bethseda (John 5:1-9), fed a crowd of at least five thousand with five small loaves and two small fish (John 6:1-15), walked on the Sea of Galilee (John 6:16-24), restored the sight of a man who had been born blind (John 9:1-7) and raised Lazarus from the dead (John 11:17-44). A case can be made for saying that John wrote his account of Jesus' life around the framework of these seven signs and the seven "I am" statements, both of which are pointers to the fact that Jesus is God.

From Mark 4:35 through to Mark 5:43, Mark records a cluster of four miracles, all of which point to Jesus' deity. They all show Jesus to be the Lord. Jesus calms the storm (Mark 4:35-41) to show that He is Lord of creation. The Creator spoke and His creation obeyed His command. Jesus heals a demon-possessed man (Mark 5:1-20) to show that He is Lord over evil. Evil had completely ruined this man's life, robbing him of his sanity, family and dignity. Jesus healed this man, restoring everything evil had stolen from him.

Jesus cured a woman who was suffering from internal bleeding (Mark 5:25-34) to show that He is Lord over disease and illness. Medical science had failed miserably to help her, but with almost effortless ease Jesus was able to give her back her health. Jesus raised a twelve-year old girl from the dead (Mark 5:21-24 and 35-43) to show that He was Lord over death. The ultimate tragedy had hit Jarius. His daughter had been ripped away from him by death, but Jesus gave her back to him.

These miracles highlight the fact that Jesus is the Lord, pointing to His deity.

The truth that Jesus is Lord is not simply a theological conviction. It challenges us to ask if Jesus is our Lord.
➤ A radical commitment to Jesus as Lord has an intellectual dimension to it. We refuse to buy into the "everybody decides for himself or herself what is true and

no one has the right to tell anyone else what to believe" attitude that is rampant in contemporary society. Instead we submit our thinking to Jesus' control. How does this happen, since Jesus is not physically present with us? Jesus teaches us through His Word (Matthew 11:29). As we allow the Bible's teaching to increasingly dominate our thinking, we show that Jesus is our Lord.

➤ A radical commitment to Jesus as Lord has a moral dimension to it. Relativism rules the roost today, not only in the area of thinking but also in the area of behaviour. So much of current behaviour is controlled by a "feel free to do whatever you want as long as it does not make you feel bad about yourself" attitude. Jesus is our Lord when we do not let relativism or our feelings drive our behaviour. Instead, out of love for Him and in the power of His Spirit, we obey Jesus' commands as found in the Bible (John 14:21). Even when it is inconvenient and difficult, makes us unpopular and causes us to say "No!" to our feelings and preferences, we are to do what Jesus says.

➤ A radical commitment to Jesus as Lord has a career dimension to it. The career choice of so many is determined by questions of finance and benefits. They only follow a career path that will rake them in a huge salary and offer them the best deal. Jesus' followers do not plan their lives as if their relationship with Jesus is somehow detached from those plans and irrelevant to them. Instead, we place our future at His disposal. We see our career as a form of service to Jesus and to others, so we only want to pursue one that advances the cause of the gospel in the world (Matthew 6:33) and helps others (Philippians 2:1-11).

4. JESUS' SINLESSNESS REINFORCED HIS CLAIM TO BE GOD

The Bible presents Jesus as someone who never sinned in any area of His life. Never once, even for a fraction of a second, did Jesus fail to love God with every part of His being, or did He break God's Law in His words, actions, thoughts or motives.

❖ **WHAT JESUS THOUGHT ABOUT HIMSELF**

Prayer played a very important part in Jesus' life. He prayed on many different occasions. Some of His prayers are recorded in the Gospels, with Matthew 11:25-26, Matthew 26:36-44, John 17:1-16 being a few examples. Jesus also taught about prayer, giving us a model prayer that we call *The Lord's Prayer* (Matthew 6:9-13 and Luke 11:2-4). In this model prayer, Jesus instructed us to ask God to forgive our sins. However, never once, do we read of Jesus asking forgiveness for Himself. Was Jesus acting as a hypocrite; pretending that something was true of Him when it clearly was not? No! Jesus hated hypocrisy and could spot it a mile away. He consistently condemned it. If He had needed to ask for forgiveness for Himself, He would have done so. The reason why He was free from all sense of sin was because He was devoid of sin in His life.

❖ **WHAT JESUS' FRIENDS THOUGHT OF HIM**

We can often be oblivious to our own faults. Our friends, who know us best, see our faults. However, Jesus' friends came to the conclusion that He was sinless (1 John 3:5, 1 Peter 1:19 and 2:22 and Hebrews 7:26). Jesus' disciples got on each other's nerves, quarrelling and squabbling all the time. However, when they compared their lives with Jesus', they did not get as much as a whiff in Jesus' character of the sins they found in themselves.

❖ **WHAT JESUS' ENEMIES THOUGHT OF HIM**

If Jesus' friends might have been biased in His favour, that was certainly not an accusation that could have been levelled against His enemies. They hated Him with a demonic ferocity.

Think of the person who most despises you. He thinks you will go far, and the further the better! Imagine if that person got the chance to publicly highlight all your faults. He would think that it was Christmas and his birthday rolled into one. He would hardly know where to begin, and he would find it hard to stop. One day, Jesus challenged them to highlight any ways in which He had sinned (John 8:46), and His enemies were silent. They would have loved to say something bad about Him, but they could not.

Jesus' sinless character does not prove His claim to be God was true. Nevertheless it strongly reinforces it. Sin is a universal complaint that infects all of us, so, if Jesus was sinless, He was not just a man, as we know men. He was distinct from us. He was supernatural.

Jesus' claim to be God is as breathtaking as it is clear. If someone today said the same sort of things about himself as Jesus did, people would say that he had delusions of megalomania. Was that the case with Jesus? His enemies thought so (John 10:20), and there were times when even His own human family came to the same conclusion (Mark 3:31-35). However, the idea that Jesus was mentally unstable has to be kicked into the long grass. There is not a shred of evidence in the accounts of His life that He was out of His mind. The picture we get of Him is that He was a universally balanced individual. His character is inconsistent with someone who is insane. "The discrepancy between the depth, sanity and shrewdness of Jesus' moral teaching and the rampant megalomania, which must lie behind His claims, has never been satisfactorily got over – unless He is indeed God" (C.S. Lewis).

SO WHAT?

Does Jesus' claim to be God really matter? It does. Bob was right when he said that Christianity centres on Jesus and His staggering assertion that He was God. The question of whether or not Jesus is God is not some side issue.

If Jesus is not God, then we have no way of knowing exactly what God is like. Just as a short-sighted person only has a blurred view of a distant object, sin has left us spiritually myopic, with, at best, only a very hazy knowledge of a distant God. Unless God Himself came to show us what He was really like, left to ourselves, we can only guess. The good news of the Christian message is that God has already come in the person of Jesus and has given us a clear picture of His character (John 14:7 and Colossians 1:15).

If Jesus is not God, we have no way of breaking free from sin. Sin has such a stranglehold on us that we cannot escape its deadly clutches. No matter how hard we try, we discover that our best is not good enough. We need someone with more than human strength, someone like God Himself, to come to our rescue. The good news of the Christian message is that God has already come in the person of Jesus to free us from sin's guilt, penalty and control (Galatians 4:4-5 and 1 Timothy 1:15).

If Jesus is not God, there is no knowledge of God and no hope of us being rescued from sin and its horrific consequences. However, because He is, there is.

DIGGING DEEPER

You might like to explore further some of the issues raised in this chapter by reading *Basic Christianity* by John Stott (Published by IVP), *Jesus Unplugged* by David Burke (Published by IVP), *Stranger than Fiction: From Manger to Megastar* by John Dickson (Published by Matthias Media), and *The Christ of the Bible and the Churches* by Geoffrey Grogan (Published by Christian Focus Publications).

4. ONE OF US

In this chapter, we are going to discover what the Bible says about Jesus' humanity.

JESUS WAS BORN JUST AS WE WERE

JESUS SUFFERED JUST AS WE DO
- Physical suffering
- Emotional suffering
- Spiritual suffering

JESUS HAD EMOTIONS JUST AS WE HAVE
- Compassion
- Anger
- Joy

JESUS WAS TEMPTED JUST AS WE ARE
- Tempted to self-gratification
- Tempted to self-glorification
- Tempted to self-assertion

BIG DEAL?
- An example to follow
- A model for mission
- A friend who understands
- An expert to help
- An advocate to plead our case

In 1996, Joan Osborne reached the charts with a song that posed the following question: "What if God was one of us?" The Bible's answer is clear. In the person of His Son, God really did become one of us. Jesus is not only 100% God, He is also 100% human. In the last chapter we explored the fact that He is fully God. In this chapter, we are going to tease out the reality of His full humanity.

Among some Christians there is a strange hesitancy to sign up to the fact that Jesus was a real human being. They are over-sensitive about Jesus' deity. They minimise Jesus' humanity because they fear that the affirmation that Jesus is 100% human might take away from the fact that He is 100% God. However, according to the Bible, the Incarnation (theological jargon for Jesus becoming a real human being) was an addition, not a subtraction. The Bible never tells us that He became God. He always existed as fully God (John 1:1). In contrast, it never says that He always existed as fully human. It states that at a precise and decisive point in time, Jesus took upon Himself a real humanity on top of His real divinity (John 1:14).

However, the Bible has no such hesitancy in stating that Jesus is fully human as well as being fully God, and it produces a whole raft of evidence underlining His real humanity.

1. JESUS WAS BORN JUST AS WE WERE

With due respect to storks and gooseberry bushes, we were born after spending roughly forty weeks inside our mother's womb, and there we developed until the moment we arrived on the planet. Jesus had similar antenatal and birth experiences. There was nothing unusual about His birth. Perhaps the innkeeper's outhouse was not as hygienic as the delivery room or theatre in which we were born, but another normal delivery occurred in Bethlehem the day Jesus was born.

This means that Jesus had a human body just like ours, with the same biochemistry, anatomy, physiology and central nervous system. His body had a genetic composition similar to our own, though of course with a specific code unique to Jesus as an individual. Jesus was not gender-neutral, neither female nor male; He was a male, and more specifically a first-century Jewish male.

Historically Christians have used the term "the Virgin Birth" to describe Jesus' arrival into the world. That term is not meant to give the impression that Jesus was born in some unnatural way. He had a completely natural birth.

What was supernatural was His conception. In their obviously independent yet strikingly harmonious accounts of Jesus' birth, both Matthew and Luke agree that Jesus was miraculously conceived (Matthew 1:18-25, Luke 1:26-56 and Luke 2:4-7). Mary found herself pregnant as a result of the Holy Spirit's activity in her womb, and not because she and Joseph were sexually active (Matthew 1:18 and 20, and Luke 1:35). The term "the Virgin Birth" includes Jesus' natural birth and His supernatural conception.

Some have found the idea of Jesus' supernatural conception hard to stomach.

➢ It is challenged on the grounds that it is biologically absurd. In terms of fixed biological laws, the idea of a woman conceiving without being inseminated, either via sexual intercourse or via artificial insemination, is absurd. Christians do not deny this. However, we maintain that the resurrection is also a biological absurdity. Naturalistic science - science that completely leaves God out of the picture and believes in a closed, mechanical universe that only operates on fixed laws – is no more sympathetic to the idea of a corpse being miraculously raised from the dead than it is to a virgin miraculously conceiving. But the Virgin Birth and the resurrection are on a par. They are both unique, supernatural, miraculous events. If God the Father can raise Jesus from the dead through the Holy Spirit's activity then surely He is perfectly capable of bringing about Jesus' conception in a virgin's womb through the Holy Spirit's activity?

➢ Some question the Virgin Birth because they feel it makes Jesus less than truly human. "To be truly human," people argue, "means that you must be procreated, and because Jesus was not procreated like us, but conceived in Mary's womb by the Holy Spirit, He cannot be truly human." They maintain that, although the doctrine of the Virgin

Birth protects Jesus' deity, it takes away from His true humanity. This objection rests upon the false assumption that only a person who has been procreated is fully human. Adam was truly human, yet he was not procreated. He was miraculously created. The Virgin Birth does not detract from Jesus' true humanity any more than Adam's miraculous creation detracts from his true humanity.

➤ Others have been sceptical about the Virgin Birth because the other New Testament writers do not explicitly mention it. The other New Testament writers are silent about it because they assumed its historicity. It was not a matter of controversy in New Testament times, so there was no need for them to write about it.

Christians are very sensitive when the idea of the Virgin Birth comes under attack. They jump to its defence because of how it relates to other truths.

➤ It supports Jesus' claim to be God. A supernatural mode of entry into the world is in line with His claim to be a supernatural person.

➤ It points to Jesus' freedom from sin. Conceived by the Holy Spirit, He did not inherit the guilty twist called "Original Sin." He was free from sin, and through the maintained sinlessness of His unflawed human nature, Jesus was able to offer the perfect sacrifice for sin when He died on the cross (John 1:36 and 1 Peter 1:18-19).

➤ It is a sign of God's judgment on human nature. Humanity needs a Saviour, but it cannot produce one. The Saviour must come from outside, and in the Incarnation God has stepped into human history to save (Luke 19:10 and 1 Timothy 1:15).

➤ It signals God's ability to change our lives. If God can

create physical life in Mary's womb, then He is perfectly capable, through the activity of the same Spirit, of creating spiritual life in our lives (John 1:12-13).

➢ It indicates that Jesus is a new beginning. He is not a development from anything that has gone before. When we trust in Jesus as our Saviour, our lives are not just patched up. We experience a new beginning, a brand new start (2 Corinthians 5:17).

2. JESUS SUFFERED JUST AS WE DO

When Jesus came to earth, He was not wrapped up in cotton wool so that He was insulated from suffering. He experienced the whole spectrum of human pain.

❖ PHYSICAL SUFFERING

We would be ravenously hungry if we had had nothing to eat for forty days and nights. So was Jesus (Matthews 4:2). Once He was so thirsty, Jesus ignored the social protocols of His day to ask a Samaritan woman for a drink of water (John 4:6-9). Often the pressure and demands of His work left Jesus dog-tired. On one occasion He was so physically shattered that He was able to sleep soundly in a boat that was being knocked about by gale-force winds and mountainous seas (Mark 4:35-41). The physical suffering He had to endure when He was executed by crucifixion was horrendous. We have sanitised the cross because it was so brutal and savage. The Roman soldiers had plaited some thorns into the shape of a crown and rammed it down onto Jesus' head. He had been flogged. He had been spat at. He had been stripped naked. Then His hands and feet had been hammered to the cross. He died a cruel, slow death from suffocation.

❖ EMOTIONAL SUFFERING

Jesus felt disappointment when His disciples were so slow to grasp who He was (John 14:9). He felt the emotion-shattering effects of death as He wept beside the grave of His friend Lazarus (John 11:35). He experienced the heart-piercing pain of betrayal as Judas handed Him over to His enemies. He knew what it was like to be alone because His closest friends deserted Him when He needed them most.

❖ SPIRITUAL SUFFERINGS

Jesus suffered most keenly in the spiritual pain He experienced. On the night before His death, as He prayed in the Garden of Gethsemane, He was given a felt foretaste of the cross. His humanity recoiled so much from the prospect of the cross that He sweated blood (Luke 22:44). Like Jesus' physical sufferings, His spiritual sufferings reached their climax on the cross. The real horror of the cross was not what Jesus suffered physically, ghastly as it was, but what He suffered spiritually. As He absorbed the full fury of God's just anger against our sin, for the first and only time His Father turned away from Him. In spiritual anguish, Jesus screamed out, "My God! My God! Why have You forsaken Me?" (Mark 15:34).

At the end of time, billions of people were scattered on a great plain before God's throne. Most shrank back from the brilliant heat before them. But some groups near the front talked heatedly – not with cringing shame, but with belligerence. "How can God judge us? How can He know about suffering?" snapped a young brunette. She ripped open a sleeve to reveal a tattooed number from a Nazi concentration camp. "We endured torture, beating, terror and death." In another group a Negro boy lowered his collar. "What about this?" he demanded, showing an ugly rope burn. "Lynched for no other crime than being black! We were suffocated in slave ships; wrenched from our loved ones; and toiled until only death gave us release." In another group a young woman stared with sullen eyes. On her head was the stamp 'Illegitimate'. "To endure my stigma," she murmured, "was beyond, beyond..." Her voice tailed off to be taken up by others. Far across the plain were hundreds of such groups. Each had a complaint against God for the evil and suffering He permitted in His world. How lucky God was to live in heaven where all was sweetness and light; where there was no weeping, no fear, no hunger and no hatred. Indeed what did God know of what people had been forced to endure in this world? After all, God leads a pretty sheltered life, they said. So each of these groups sent out a leader, chosen because he had suffered the most. There was a Jew, a Negro, an untouchable from India, an illegitimate, a horribly deformed arthritic, a person from Hiroshima, the victim of a terrorist car bomb and a refugee whose village had been ethnically cleansed. In the centre of the plain they consulted with each other. At last they were ready to present their case. It was rather simple. Before God would be qualified to be their judge, He must endure what they endured. Their decision was that God should be sentenced to live on earth as a man. But, because He was God, they set certain safeguards to make sure He did not use His divine powers to help Himself. Let Him be born a Jew. Let the legitimacy of His birth be doubted so that no one will really know who His father is. Give Him a work to do so that even His family will think He is mad when He tries to do it. Let Him describe what no one has ever seen, tasted or smelled. Let Him describe God to man. Let Him be betrayed by His dearest friends. Let Him be indicted on false charges, tried before a prejudiced jury, and convicted by a cowardly judge. Let Him experience what it means to be completely alone, totally abandoned by every living thing. Let Him be tortured and let Him die. Let Him die so that there can be no doubt that He died. Let there be a great crowd to witness His humiliation and to verify His death.

As each leader announced his bit of the sentence, loud murmurs of approval went up from the assembled crowd. When the last had finished pronouncing sentence, there was a long silence. Those who had spoken their judgement against God left quietly. No one uttered a word. No one spoke. No one moved. For suddenly all knew – *God has already served His sentence!*

3. JESUS HAD EMOTIONS JUST AS WE HAVE

Having emotions is part and parcel of being human. So, as someone who was genuinely human, Jesus too had emotions.

❖ COMPASSION

This is the emotion most frequently attributed to Jesus. The sight of a large hungry crowd (Mark 8:2-3), or a man with leprosy (Mark 1:41), or two blind men (Matthew 20:34), or a widow whose only son had just died (Luke 7:13) moved Jesus' heart of love. When He saw that the masses were like "sheep without a shepherd," with no one to give them true spiritual guidance, He had compassion on them (Mark 6:34). He wept aloud over Jerusalem's stubborn refusal to accept Him (Luke 19:41).

❖ ANGER

When He came face-to-face with the crass commercial exploitation of religion (John 2:13-16), the nauseating hypocrisy of the religious leaders of His day, the devastating effects of sin, or even the self-important snobbery of His disciples (Mark 10:13-14), Jesus was moved to righteous anger.

❖ JOY

Although we are never told that Jesus laughed and although the Bible calls Jesus a "man of sorrows" (Isaiah 53:3), it would be wrong to think that His life was all doom and gloom. Jesus experienced joy. His delight was to do what God wanted (Psalm 40:8). He spoke of His own joy and His desire that His followers might experience it (John 15:11 and 17:13). We tend to feel joy when things are going well for us, but the moment life gets tough we get grumpy. Jesus' joy, however, was not controlled by His circumstances. What brought Him joy was His awareness of who He was, what He came to earth to do, and that He would succeed in His mission because of who He was.

4.   JESUS WAS TEMPTED JUST AS WE ARE

Being fully God, Jesus could not sin, but that does not mean He was not tempted. Jesus experienced the same temptations as we do (Hebrews 4:15). His temptations in the Judean Desert highlight this (Matthew 4:1-11 and Luke 4:1-13).

He was tempted to disobey God through self-gratification. Satan wanted Jesus to look after Number One by putting His physical needs before His spiritual needs (Matthew 4:3-4 and Luke 4:3-4). Jesus was tempted to disobey God through self-glorification. Satan tempted Jesus to draw attention to Himself rather than drawing people's attention to His Father (Matthew 4:5-7 and Luke 4:9-12).

Jesus was tempted to disobey God through self-assertion. Both Matthew and Luke write about Jesus' temptations immediately after the story of His baptism (Matthew 3:13-17 and Luke 3:21-22). One way of looking at Jesus' baptism is that it was like a press conference at which a public announcement was made that the Father's plan for Jesus' life was for Him to go to the cross to die as a substitute for His people. The allusion to Isaiah 42:1 in what the Father said (the end of Matthew 3:17 and Luke 3:22) indicates this. In return for going the way of the cross, the Father promised Jesus universal worship. This is the point of the throwback to Psalm 2:7-9 in the Father's words "This is My Son" (Matthew 3:17) and "You are My Son" (Luke 3:22). When Satan tempted Jesus to bow down before him, he was offering Him universal worship without the cross. Pressure was being put on Jesus to do His own thing and selfishly abandon His Father's plan for His life - the glory of universal worship via the pain of the cross. Satan wanted Jesus to assert Himself by rejecting His Father's right to tell Him what to do.

Those are the same temptations we face day after day. Each temptation we face can be boiled down to either self-gratification, self-glorification or self-assertion.

Although the Bible stresses that Jesus experienced the same temptations as we do, He experienced them to a greater intensity than we ever will. What happens when we are tempted? We give in. What happens if we do throw up some resistance? Satan turns the screw a little bit tighter, and then we give in. What happens if we still resist temptation? Satan turns the screw even tighter, and then we give in. We never experience the full intensity of temptation because we give in to it. Like sandcastles on the beach, we crumble long before Satan has to unleash the full force of temptation or his subtlest enticement upon us. Jesus, however, never gave in to temptation. He "has been tempted in every way, just as we are – *yet … without sin*" (Hebrews 4:15). No matter how tightly Satan turned the screw, Jesus never buckled. When Jesus was lashed and battered with hurricane-force temptations, He stood firm. He experienced an intensity of temptation that none of us will ever experience because He never gave in.

When I bought my first computer, one of my friends sent me a postcard with this message: "To err is human, but to make a real mess you need a computer!" If to err is human and Jesus did not sin, is He truly human? Joan Osborne's song raises this question because she asks, "What if God was one of us? *Just a slob like one of us?*" The Bible handles this objection to Jesus' true humanity by pointing out that the idea "to err is human" is wrong. To be truly human is not to sin. Adam, before the Fall, shows this. Adam was truly human before he sinned, and he was perfect. To sin is to be sub-human. It was only after he headed down the road of self-gratification, self-glorification and self-assertion, that Adam's humanity went into free-fall. If Jesus had been "a slob like one of us," then, rather than being truly human, He would have been sub-human. To be truly human is to love God with all our heart, soul, mind and strength. The only person who has

> ever done this is Jesus. Sin is dehumanising, but God's salvation, which recreates us into Jesus' likeness, alone makes us truly human.

BIG DEAL?

The fact that Jesus was one of us, like all the truths of the Bible, is designed to impact our lives.

❖ **AN EXAMPLE TO FOLLOW** (1 Peter 2:21)

The bracelet my youngest daughter bought was emblazoned with the letters "WWJD". I asked her what the letters stood for. After giving me her 'why-do-dads-always-ask-such-stupid-questions' look, she sighed and replied, "What would Jesus do." Here is a fundamental principle for Christian living. Before every action, thought or word, we are to ask ourselves the question, "What would Jesus do in a similar situation?" Then we are to follow His example. How do we know what Jesus would do in any given situation? The Bible alone tells us.

❖ **A MODEL FOR MISSION** (John 1:14 and Philippians 2:6-8)

When Jesus came to earth, His life was not one of sanitised detachment but of involvement. He lived where He could see human sin, hear human swearing and blasphemy, come into contact with human disease and experience human poverty and squalor. He not only shared our nature; He also shared our environment. He lived a real life in the real world. We are to copy Jesus' model of reaching out to His sin-ravaged world as we reach out to our sin-ravaged world. We cannot effectively reach the poor, disadvantaged and deprived with the good news about Jesus from a distance. We need to engage with our communities. In His mission, Jesus did that, getting along-side people and sharing their environment. In our mission, we are to do the same.

❖ **A FRIEND WHO UNDERSTANDS** (Hebrews 4:14-16)

Several years ago, I was speaking to a group of students in a teacher training college in north Dublin. I was talking about how God understands all that we go through. One of the students interrupted me. "How can God understand?" he asked. "He is up there and we are down here. God is so removed from the real world and from true human experience that He cannot possibly understand what we are going through". I pointed out that God really does understand because, in Jesus, God Himself became a real man and lived a real life, experiencing everything that we are exposed to as human beings. The term the Bible uses is that Jesus "sympathises" with us (Hebrews 4:15). Among other things, Jesus' sympathy means that, because He had a real humanity, He understands exactly what we go through day-by-day. Sometimes we feel that no one understands what we are going through. Jesus does, and because He does, He invites us to go to Him and ask Him for the strength to handle our pressures and difficulties in a way that brings honour to Him (Hebrews 4:16). When life is a lemon and we want our money back, we ask, "Why me?" Part of Jesus' answer is "I know what it's like for I've been there too!"

❖ **AN EXPERT TO HELP** (Hebrews 2:18)

When we want help with something, we ask an expert. When Joan, my wife, experienced problems designing a web-site for her Master of Science project, she asked her project supervisor, who was an expert in web design, for help. If we want help to overcome temptation, we need to ask an expert, and the only expert in overcoming temptation is Jesus. He has experienced the whole spectrum of temptation to its fiercest intensity and overcome it, so He is able to help us. Temptation does not have to defeat us. Through the activity of His Holy Spirit in our minds and hearts, showing us the escape route out of our temptation (1 Corinthians 10:13) and giving us the inner strength, Jesus helps us to beat temptation.

❖ **AN ADVOCATE TO PLEAD OUR CASE** (Hebrews 4:15-16 and 1 John 2:1-2)

A youth worker asked some teenagers what they did when they were tempted. A sixteen-year-old boy with a challenged waistline immediately replied, "I eat it!" The whole group roared with laughter, except for one fifteen-year-old. She brought the laughter to a sudden halt by saying, "When I am tempted, I give in." Jesus wants us to beat temptation (1 John 2:1a), but the tragedy is that we do not utilise His help when we are tempted. We give in and sin. We need forgiveness. However, there is hope for failures like us. Jesus has taken His humanity back into heaven with Him, and He pleads our cause with the Father when we sin (Hebrews 4:15-16). He secures our forgiveness, not on the basis of what we have done, but on the basis of what He has done (1 John 2:1b-2a).

DIGGING DEEPER

You might like to explore further some of the issues raised in this chapter by reading *The Beauty of Jesus* by Clifford Pond (Published by Grace Publications), *The Man who Made the Millennium* by John Blanchard (Published by Evangelical Press), and *How did Jesus feel?* By Jim Mayhew (Published by Christian Focus Publications).

5. GREAT EXPECTATIONS

> **In this chapter, we are going to discover what the Bible says about Jesus' work as Prophet, Priest and King.**
> GOD'S FINAL PROPHET
> GOD'S GREAT PRIEST
> • **Jesus is the only go-between**
> • **Jesus is the perfect sacrifice for sin**
> • **Jesus is the present intercessor**
> GOD'S PERFECT KING
> • **Jesus' Kingdom is spiritual**
> • **Jesus' Kingdom is universal**

What is Jesus' surname? Hands up everyone who said, "Christ." Sorry, that is the wrong answer. Jesus' legal father was Joseph (Matthew 1:16, Luke 3:23 and John 6:42), so His surname was "son of Joseph" (John 1:45). The name "Doctor" does not appear on my brother's birth certificate. It was a title given to him later on to indicate his line of work. In the same way, "Christ" is not one of Jesus' names but a title giving us the big picture of what He came to do. Before we examine some of the details, we are going to think about this title as it opens up a window through which we can get a broad overview of Jesus' work.

To understand what this title means we have to go back to the Old Testament. "Christ" is the Greek equivalent of the Hebrew word "Messiah," and both terms literally mean "the Anointed One." A flick through the historical bits of the Old Testament will reveal that three groups of people were anointed to carry out a task for God – prophets (1 Kings 19:16 and 1 Chronicles 16:22), priests (Exodus 28:41, 30:30 40:13 and 40:15) and kings (1 Samuel 16:1-13, 1 Kings 1:34 and 2 Kings 9:6). So when the Bible says that Jesus is the Christ, it is saying that He carries out these three roles.

1. GOD'S FINAL PROPHET

Although the term conjures up in our minds a pundit who predicts the future, the Bible's job description for a prophet actually included much more. His main task was to act as God's spokesman, receiving messages directly from Him. Ninety-nine times in the Old Testament prophetic books we run across the expression "the word of the Lord came to" such-and-such a prophet. Then he passed on what God had told him to the people. The prophets' catchphrase was "this is what the Lord says." They were God's mouthpieces; not giving their own opinions but authoritatively telling people what God wanted them to know. At times, there was a future aspect to their messages. However, often it was a matter of taking what God had already said and showing its contemporary relevance.

In spite of the fact that the Prophetic Hall of Fame included big-hitters such as Elijah, Elisha, Isaiah, Jeremiah and Ezekiel, the Old Testament held out the prospect that, one day, God would send one final prophet who would be in a league of His own. This expectation was fuelled in particular by Deuteronomy 18:15 and 18. The New Testament writers saw Jesus as the fulfilment of this Old Testament strand of thought, presenting Him as God's prophet *par excellence*. In one of his sermons, Peter applies the Deuteronomy 18 statements about the coming prophet to Jesus (Acts 3:22). Stephen did the same during his trial before the Sanhedrin (Acts 7:37). The writer of the book of Hebrews follows suit (Hebrew 1:1-2). He links how God spoke in the past through the prophets and how God spoke definitively through Jesus, signalling the fact that the writer saw Jesus as being the last and greatest in the long line of prophets.

Jesus Himself was aware that He had a prophetic role. He did all the things a prophet did – applying God's Law to the contemporary situation (Matthew 15:1-9 and 21:15-17) and making predictions about the future (Matthew 24:1-51, Mark 13:1-36 and Luke 19:41-44). He claimed that He was speaking God's words (John 8:28 and 12:49-50). He even referred to Himself as a prophet (Mark 6:4 and Luke 13:33).

> ➤ Jesus was way out in front of the Old Testament prophets, and this is seen in the catchphrase Jesus used. The Old Testament prophets prefaced their prophetic announcements with the statement "This is what the Lord says," the emphasis falling on the word "Lord." Jesus' catchphrase was "I tell you the truth," or as the King James Version quaintly puts it "Verily, verily, I say unto thee," the emphasis falling on the word "I." The Old Testament prophets realised they spoke *from* God. Jesus was conscious He spoke *as* God.
>
> ➤ The fact that Jesus is ahead of the Old Testament prophets is also seen in the way people reacted to what He said. When people heard Him speak, they were bowled over by His authority (Matthew 7:29 and Mark 1:22). They had yawned their way through many a sermon, but when Jesus preached, the people sat up and paid attention. They had never heard anything like it. Jesus' authority overwhelmed them. Unlike the teachers of the law, when He spoke about God and spiritual matters, He seemed to know what He was talking about from firsthand experience.

We must not think that this business of Jesus being a prophet is just long ago and far away stuff. He still exercises a prophetic role today, speaking to us, not in person, but through His Word. This is why so much emphasis is placed on Christians reading the Bible and thinking over what it says. It is as the Holy Spirit helps us to understand the Bible's meaning and relevance to our contemporary situation that we hear Jesus' voice.

BEING "ON MESSAGE"

If Jesus, God's final Prophet, tells us what He wants us to believe and how He wants us to live through the Bible, how can we make sure that we are "on message", listening to

Him?

➤ Find a time. Everyone's schedule is different and they even vary from day to day. We need to find a time that suits us; when we are most awake and able to concentrate, and when we will be most undisturbed.

➤ Get a place. Read the Bible in a place that we associate with thinking and reflection. Reading the Bible in bed is not recommended because we associate our beds with sleeping and not with studying.

➤ Have a system. Nutritionalists are always at us about the need to eat a balanced diet so that we might stay healthy. Spiritual health is promoted by having a balanced spiritual diet. We need to be familiar with all parts of the Bible. To do that, we need to have a system. If we do not have a system, we will only read the bits of the Bible we like. Bible reading notes, which are available in Christian bookshops, will get us to read all parts of the Bible.

➤ Use a method. We can fall into the trap of reading the notes instead of reading the Bible. The best way to sidestep that trap is to ask the Bible passage questions *before* we read the comments in the Bible reading notes.

☑ What do these verses teach me about God the Father, Jesus, the Holy Spirit, salvation, and the church?

☑ What does this passage teach me about myself and my relationship with God?

☑ In these verses is there a command to obey, a sin to avoid, a promise to believe or an example to follow?

☑ Does this passage contain a principle for Christian living?

2. GOD'S GREAT PRIEST

The pivotal figure of Old Testament religion was the priest. Chunks of the opening books of the Old Testament are given over to describing in minute detail the work the priest was to do. When all the instructions are boiled down, the priest was to act as a go-between between God and human beings. The New Testament writers, especially the writer of the book of Hebrews, use what the Old Testament has to say about the priest to explain who Jesus is and what He did and still does. They saw the figure of the Old Testament priest as pointing forward to Jesus.

❖ JESUS IS THE ONLY GO-BETWEEN

The Old Testament priest's mediation in the disagreement between God and people was imperfect. As a human being, he could really only understand the human side of things, and, because he was not divine, he could not adequately represent God. A good go-between must be able to represent the interests of both sides in a dispute. The Old Testament priest's imperfect mediation anticipated the arrival of the ideal go-between who could represent the interests of both God and people because he was both human and divine. The New Testament announces that with the coming of Jesus, who is uniquely 100% God and 100% human in the same person, the perfect and only go-between has arrived (1 Timothy 2:5). Jesus was conscious of His own unique mediation role. In John 14:6, He stated categorically that He was the only way to God. "I am *the* Way (not *a* way)," He said, and just in case we failed to pick up what He was getting at, He added, "no one comes to the Father *except through Me*".

If Christians said that Jesus was just one of several legitimate routes to God, most people would be happy. It is our insistence that Jesus alone is the way to God that causes people to cry "Foul!" and to slam us for being intolerant bigots. In our pluralistic society, how would you go about sticking up for the Bible's stance on Jesus being the only go-between? If you are not sure, read John Stott's robust but gracious defence of the Bible's position in a chapter titled "The Uniqueness of Jesus Christ" in his book

64

❖ JESUS IS THE PERFECT SACRIFICE FOR SIN

Right from the word go, certainly from the story of Cain and Abel (Genesis 4:1-16), God made it clear that people could not approach Him to worship in any way they fancied. He could only be approached if blood was spilt in death. There was no debate about this; it was the rule of engagement that God drew up. On the back of this principle, a sacrificial system was put in place so that people in Old Testament times could worship God.

The worshipper realised that, in and of himself, he cannot approach God. God is holy, pure and perfect. He is sinful, impure and twisted. If he is to approach God, a sacrifice must be made. So he brought his animal, very often a flawless lamb, to the altar. He placed his hands on the animal's head and confessed his sin. In this act, his sin was symbolically transferred to the animal. He knew that he deserved to die because he had violated God's law (Ezekiel 18:4), but he transferred his guilt and liability for punishment to a substitute, who would die in his place. Then he killed the animal. (Old Testament religion was not for the squeamish, who got light headed at the sight of tomato juice.) Death was what the worshipper deserved because he had sinned. However, the death sentence was inflicted on his substitute.

Finally the priest sprinkled the animal's blood on various parts of the altar and burnt the carcass. (In some of the Old Testament sacrifices, the whole of the carcass was incinerated, while in others only certain parts of the animal were burnt). It was not until the priest had done his work that the worshipper's sin was dealt with and he could approach God (Leviticus 17:11). If blood was not spilt and a sacrifice offered up on the altar, the problem of sin was still not sorted out.

The New Testament writers see Jesus as fulfilling the Old Testament sacrificial system. Jesus was the perfect Lamb (John 1:29 and 1 Peter 1:19). When He died, our sin was transferred to Jesus and He was punished for it (2 Corinthians 5:21). There is forgiveness for us because Jesus' blood was spilt (Hebrews 9:22).

However, the main problem with the Old Testament sacrificial system was that it really could not deal effectively with sin. The sacrifices had to be repeated day after day, week after week, year after year and even century after century. Generations of priests carried out the same ritual. The hope grew that, one day, God would send a great priest who would offer up such a sacrifice that it would completely deal with the problem of human sin. The writer of the book of Hebrews picks up this hope and presents Jesus as the great priest *par excellence*. It was impossible for animals' blood to successfully deal with human sin (Hebrews 10:4), but Jesus' voluntary offering up of Himself does effectively take care of sin (Hebrews 10:10). In contrast to the Old Testament sacrifices that were repeated daily, Jesus offered up an unrepeated "once for all" sacrifice (Hebrews 10:1-2). In contrast to the Old Testament priests who offer up an animal, Jesus offered up Himself (Hebrews 10:10). In His death, He simultaneously acted as the priest and the victim. In contrast to the Old Testament priests who never sat down because their work was never finished, Jesus "sat down at the right hand of the majesty in heaven" to indicate that His sacrificial work was finished (Hebrews 1:3).

❖ JESUS IS THE PRESENT INTERCESSOR

Jesus still carries out a priestly role today. The focus has changed. Today He no longer offers Himself up as a sacrifice. That phase of Jesus' priestly activity is complete. Instead He intercedes for us in heaven (Romans 8:34 and Hebrews 7:25). By Jesus' intercession, the Bible means Jesus' intervention with the Father on our behalf. It comes into play at specific times in our lives.

When we are tempted We have not got what it takes to defeat temptation. Trying to stand firm against it in our own pathetically weak resources is a recipe for failure. We need outside help. Jesus encourages us to go to Him for it. He will pray for us, asking the Father to give us the Spirit's assistance so that we will be able to say an emphatic "No!" to temptation (Hebrews

2:18 and 4:15-16).

When we sin God's game plan for us is that we do not give in to temptation and sin (1 Thessalonians 4:7 and 1 John 2:1a). However, God realises that we will blow it and sin will get the better of us. When that happens, Jesus intervenes on our behalf with the Father (1 John 2:1-2), acting like a defence lawyer. On several occasions, I have been asked by a defence lawyer to write a character reference to a court on behalf of someone who is on trial. I have usually written about the defendant's good behaviour in the past, and asked the judge to show leniency because what the defendant did was totally out of character. The focus of my letters to the court was the defendant's character. However, when Jesus, our defence lawyer, asks the Father to forgive us for our sin, He does not focus His plea on our characters. If He did, we would have no hope of experiencing God's forgiveness. Instead He reminds the Father that He died for us, and, on the basis of His death, God forgives us.

When we have to do something for God Sooner or later, God will ask us to do something for Him. It might be to speak to a friend about Jesus, or to help out with something in the church. Our initial reaction is "No. I have not got the ability or the experience". However, Jesus reassures us of His gracious power to help us do what God wants (2 Corinthians 12:9). The interesting thing about Jesus' promised help is that He gives it to us *as* we do what God wants. We say to Him, "Jesus, when I've experienced Your power, then I'll do what God wants". Jesus says to us, "You've got it the wrong way round. You do what God wants and as you do it you will experience My power."

The exciting thing about the way Jesus pleads our case with the Father is that the Father always goes along with what Jesus wants. The Father delights in His Son because of who He is and what He has done, and so always gives Him what He asks. Jesus' intercession guarantees that we will get help when we are tempted, forgiveness when we sin, and power when we have to do something for God.

The New Testament informs us that all Christians are priests (1 Peter 2:9, Revelation 1:6 and Revelation 5:10) in that we offer up sacrifices to God. Obviously our sacrifices are different from Jesus' sacrifice. With the best will in the world, we cannot deal with sin. The sacrifices we offer to God are spiritual (1 Peter 2:5).

➤ Lives lived for God and His glory (Romans 12:1). We compartmentalize life into the spiritual and the ordinary. We think that those who live their lives in a religious context, such as ministers and missionaries, are living more spiritual lives than those who live their lives in the marketplace or the home. The Bible does not make this distinction between the sacred and the secular. We are to see everything we do as service to God and are to do it for His glory (Ephesians 6:6-8 and Colossians 3:2).

➤ Giving to Christian work (Philippians 4:19). Christian giving is not like Income Tax, which we pay because we have to and about which we are always moaning. Giving to Christian work is a joyful act of worship to God (2 Corinthians 8:5 and 9:7).

➤ Thankfulness (Hebrews 13:15). In our society, thankfulness is in short supply. People find "Thank you" two of the hardest words to say. Today people put a premium on their rights. They have a right to everything, so why should they say thanks to anyone who gives them what is theirs by right? Christians are to be different. We are to be grateful to God and others for all they do for us, constantly expressing that gratitude to them.

➤ Doing good to others (Hebrews 13:16). Jesus taught that pleasing God has two sides to it – loving God with everything we have and loving other people in the same way as we love ourselves (Mark 12:30-31). We must not drive a

wedge between these two aspects of pleasing God by
neglecting the second in our pursuit of the first.

3. GOD'S PERFECT KING

In the first phase of its history, Israel had no human king.
God was Israel's king. However, God's people felt the squeeze of
peer pressure and asked God for a human king like all the
neighbouring nations. God agreed (1 Samuel 8:1-22), as it had
been part of His plan for His people that they should be ruled
over by a king of His choice (Deuteronomy 17:14-20). However,
God expected the way Israel's kings reigned to be a mirror image
of how He ruled over His people. Israel's kings were to rule in
righteousness, to frame laws that were in line with God's Law, to
judge the people with rigorous impartiality, to encourage his
subjects to follow his example of honouring God, to bring peace
to his people's lives, and to unite the people in God's service.

This was mission impossible for Israel's kings. David, the
greatest of Israel's kings, came closest, but even he was not all
that he should have been. After David's death, things went
downhill all the way. David's successors were a motley lot. It is
true that some of them (Asa, Jehosaphat, Joash, Uzziah, Jotham,
Hezekiah and Josiah) were not too bad, but most of them were
downright awful and some were absolutely dire. They turned the
idea of Israel's king reflecting God's rule on its head. People
began to think that there must be something better than this.

The prospect that in the future God would send the perfect
king who would replicate God's rule in his rule was heightened by
God's promise to David that one of his descendants would rule
over His people forever (2 Samuel 7:16) and Old Testament
passages such as Isaiah 9:6-7, Ezekiel 34:1-16 (Israel's kings were
referred to as shepherds of God's flock), Micah 5:2 and 4 that
predicted the coming of this perfect king.

Over and over again the New Testament presents Jesus as
that promised King. The news of Jesus' birth is couched in terms
of an announcement of a royal birth (Luke 1:31-33, Luke 2:11

and Matthew 2:2). From a human point of view, Jesus' family tree can be traced back to David (Matthew 1:1-17 and Luke 3:23-38). He also fulfils God's promise to David by being born in Bethlehem, David's hometown (Luke 2:1-7). Jesus' preferred self-designation was the title "the Son of Man." As we have seen that title has its roots in Daniel 7:13-14. Not only is Daniel's Son of Man a divine figure, He was also a royal figure. The central theme of Jesus' preaching was "the Kingdom of God." (Matthew prefers to call it "the Kingdom of heaven.") Jesus announced that God's Kingdom was at hand because He, the King, had arrived. The way He and His followers paraded into Jerusalem on the Sunday before His crucifixion not only sent shockwaves reverberating around the Jewish religious and political establishment, it also fulfilled Old Testament prophecy about God's perfect King arriving in Jerusalem riding on a donkey (Matthew 21:1-17 and Zechariah 9:9). He was executed for claiming to be a king (John 19:19). Jesus reigns in heaven as the King, who has returned to his throne after defeating His enemies (Psalm 2:6-9, Psalm 24:7-10, Revelation 5:5 and Revelation 7:17). One day, when He returns, everyone will know beyond a shadow of doubt that Jesus is God's perfect King (Revelation 19:16).

Although Jesus certainly considered Himself as God's perfect King, He was not the type of king people expected Him to be. Popular expectation, which was shaped more by Jewish nationalism than by the Old Testament, was that God's coming King would be a military and political figure who would restore Israel's glory days by sweeping the hated Roman occupying forces out of the country and so re-establish Israel's independence. Jesus did not buy into that idea of kingship (John 18:36), and quickly got offside when the masses tried to force Him into that mould (John 6:14-15).

❖ JESUS' KINGDOM IS SPIRITUAL

We use the word "kingdom" to mean either a physically definable geographical area, or the people, over whom a monarch reigns. So the United Kingdom is either the large island and the northwest part of the smaller island situated on the western end of Europe, or it is the area over which Queen Elizabeth II reigns. Jesus' Kingdom is not a geographical territory, but Jesus' rule over people's lives; a relationship rather than a place. It exists wherever people place their lives under His control and, as a result, experience His forgiveness and freedom (Colossians 1:13-14). It is inward and invisible (Luke 17:20-21), focusing on the spiritual rather than the material and physical (Romans 14:17).

In the whole of Matthew 5-7, a section of the Bible popularly referred to as 'The Sermon on the Mount,' Jesus sets out what matters should concern those who are citizens of His Kingdom. In Matthew 5:3-10, a passage known as 'The Beatitudes,' Jesus brings these matters into sharp focus.

➢ As citizens of Jesus' Kingdom we will not be self-confident but instead be totally dependant on God's grace. We will do this because we realise that we are spiritually bankrupt and that our own natural resources are at rock-bottom (Matthew 5:3).

➢ As citizens of Jesus' Kingdom we will be sensitive about sin's presence in our lives. It will cause us pain when we fail to be the people God expects us to be (Matthew 5:4).

➢ Like Jesus our meek King, we will gladly embrace God's will for our lives even when it will cause us inconvenience and suffering, and we will lovingly stoop to serve others (Matthew 5:5).

➢ Unlike people all around us who live for money, power, pleasure or happiness, as citizens of Jesus' Kingdom we will have a ravenous appetite and an unquenchable thirst to know God better, to live close to Him, and to become increasingly like Jesus (Matthew 5:6).

➢ As citizens of Jesus' Kingdom we will have a compassion

71

for those in need that will lead to activity to relieve their need (Matthew 5:7). In particular, we will turn our backs on the idea that "we do not get mad – we get even". Our experience of God's forgiveness makes us want to forgive those who have hurt us.

➤ In a world obsessed with image and looking good, as citizens of Jesus' Kingdom we will not be contented with outward appearance. We will also go after inward purity (Matthew 5:8). We will want nothing ugly and self-centred to corrupt our thoughts, motives and attitudes, or our actions and words.

➤ For citizens of Jesus' Kingdom being insulted, misrepresented, marginalized, physically attacked, laughed at and verbally assaulted goes with the territory (Matthew 5:10-11 and 2 Timothy 3:12). We will not retaliate or become bitter. Strange as it sounds, we will rejoice (Matthew 5:12 and James 1:2) because the opposition of those who are not Christians shows us that we really are citizens of Jesus' Kingdom (John 15:19) with heaven as our destination.

Jesus' Kingdom breaks into people's lives and its values and lifestyle develop in their lives, not as a result of military revolution or political legislation or social agitation, but by spiritual means such as preaching (Acts 8:12, Acts 19:18 and Acts 28:31) and prayer (Matthew 6:10).

❖ JESUS' KINGDOM IS UNIVERSAL

Jesus has been given the supreme position of authority in the universe (Matthew 28:18 and Philippians 2:9-11). There is not a square millimetre of this universe that does not announce that Jesus is King. He controls the lives of the individual, the decisions of political leaders and governments and the history of nations on behalf of His people (Ephesians 1:20-22). His strategy is to save His people, make them increasingly like Him, and bring them safely to be with Him heaven (Ephesians 5:25b-27). He will carry out His plan (Philippians 1:6); nothing can stop Him (Daniel 4:35).

Yet that does not appear to be the way things are in the world, for rather than Jesus being in control, it seems as if Satan is running the show. Many governments pass legislation that is blatantly against what the Bible teaches, and some encourage the persecution of Christians. We all know of people who want nothing to do with Jesus. Although we say that Jesus has set us free from sin's control, we sin every day. It looks as if what is going on all around us and in us is at odds with the Bible's bold assertion that Jesus rules over everywhere and everyone.

How do we square the circle between what the Bible teaches about Jesus' universal kingly rule and what we see happening in the world? The simple answer is to say that the Bible has got it wrong, but that 'solution' is a non-starter for the Christian. The Bible resolves the tension by pointing out that although Jesus' universal kingly rule has been established and is a reality, it has not yet been perfectly realised. On 6th June 1944, the Allies launched "Operation Overlord", and British, Canadian and American troops stormed ashore on the beaches of Normandy. As far as the struggle against Nazism was concerned, D-day was the defining moment of World War II, for once the Allies had established that beachhead in Hitler's "Fortress Europe", the war was effectively over. However, D-day was not VE (Victory in Europe)-day as it took many months of bitter fighting, many casualties and some major setbacks before the Nazi forces surrendered on 8th May 1945. When He died and rose again, Jesus' Kingdom had its D-day. This was the defining moment of human history, when Satan was decisively defeated and Jesus' rule over everything and everyone was established. However, the Kingdom's VE-day is still in the future, and that will only happen when Jesus returns (Revelation 11:15). We live in the period between the Kingdom's D-day and VE-day, and this is a period characterised by struggle and spiritual combat as the forces of

73

darkness lash out in a futile attempt to delay their inevitable defeat. The tension between what the Bible teaches about Jesus' universal kingly rule and what we see happening in the world is explained by the fact that we are living in this *already but not yet* period, in which Jesus' universal reign has been established and is a reality but has not been perfectly realised.

> If Jesus is King of our individual lives, then we ought to obey Him. Jesus is not a constitutional monarch with no real power. He is like an ancient king, who expected his subjects to ask "How high?" when he said, "Jump!". I know that in our I-am-only-going-to-do-what-I-want-to-do society "obey" is a four-letter word, but out of love for Him and in response to all He has done for us, Jesus expects us to obey Him (John 14:15). The commands Jesus gives us are designed to fill our lives with blessing, not to short-change us (John 10:10). As we do what Jesus says, far from our lives being blighted and stunted, we will enjoy an ever-deepening experience of God's love, joy and peace (John 14:21 and 23).

> If Jesus is King of our world, then we ought to be making His kingship known. We are to make the invisible Kingdom visible through our words and lives. We are to tell others that the King has come and that, on the basis of His death and resurrection, He offers a right relationship with God that leads to an experience of joy and peace for anyone who submits to His control (Matthew 24:14 and Romans 14:17). We are to make our message credible by displaying the reality of Kingdom life in our lifestyle and relationships.

> If Jesus is King of the church, then His Word must be the only factor that controls our corporate behaviour. Although in theory we say that in the church Jesus rules, sometimes in practice He does not get a look-in. Instead of

Jesus calling the shots, tradition and pragmatism dictate what goes on in the church. It is the "we-have-always-done-it-this-way-and-will-always-do-it-this-way-world-without-end-amen" or the "we-cannot-do-that-because-it-might-offend-someone-and-make-people-feel-unhappy" options that are listened to. The question of what does Jesus say in the Bible about this matter is, at best, relegated to a poor second place, but more probably not even taken on board in our decision making.

Samuel Beckett's play *Waiting for Godot* takes place in a music hall where Estragon and Vladimir, the play's central characters, wait for the arrival of someone called Godot. But Godot never makes it. The Old Testament anticipated the arrival of someone who would be God's final Prophet, God's great Priest and God's perfect King. At times this expectation burned brightly, while at other times it faded. Then, with the entrance of Jesus on to the stage of history, the New Testament writers announced that 'Godot' had arrived. The great Old Testament expectation was now fulfilled.

DIGGING DEEPER

You might like to explore further some of the issues raised in this chapter by reading *The Unfolding Mystery* by Edmund Clowney (Published by P&R), *The Root and Branch* by Joseph A Pipa (Published by Christian Focus Publications), and *Look to the Rock* by Alec Motyer (Published by IVP)

6. CROSS PURPOSES

In this chapter, we are going to discover what the Bible says about Jesus' death.
JESUS' DEATH SECURED FOR US A RIGHT RELATIONSHIP WITH GOD
- **Jesus' death – satisfying God's justice**
- **Jesus' death – displaying God's love**

JESUS' DEATH SECURED OUR FREEDOM
JESUS' DEATH SECURED RENEWED FRIENDSHIP BETWEEN GOD AND US
MAKING THE CONNECTION
- **Repentance**
- **Faith**

You're feeling hungry, but help is at hand. Up ahead is a large yellow M-shaped sign. There is a McDonald's nearby. Soon you are tucking into a Big Mac and that hollow feeling in your stomach has disappeared. You are watching your favourite team play. You immediately know that they are wearing Adidas sportswear from the three stripes on the team's kit. Every business and organisation has its distinctive logo. Even religions and ideologies have their own immediately recognisable symbols. Islam has the crescent moon, while Marxism's symbol is the hammer and sickle. Christianity is no exception. It has its logo or symbol - the cross. The cross was not the earliest Christian symbol; that honour belongs to the fish. The Greek word for "fish" was an acronym for "Jesus Christ, Son of God, Saviour". However, the cross gradually ousted the fish, and it became the universally accepted logo of Christianity.

Christianity had its roots in Judaism and the first civilisation it significantly impacted was that of the Roman Empire. So, in the light of the horror with which both the Jews and Romans regarded crucifixion, the choice of the cross as the symbol of Christianity is very surprising. The

76

Romans executed traitors, criminals, slaves and other forms of low-life by crucifixion, but never Roman citizens. Cicero, a contemporary of Julius Caesar, expressed how the Romans viewed crucifixion: "To bind a Roman citizen is a crime; to flog Him is an abomination; to kill him is almost an act of murder; to crucify him is - what? There is no fitting word that can possibly describe so horrible a deed!" The Jews found crucifixion equally offensive. For them, to be crucified was to die under God's curse (Deuteronomy 21:23), and, for a Jew, nothing was more abhorrent than that. Nevertheless, the early Christians adopted this logo of shame, disdain and scorn as the symbol of their faith. (A modern equivalent would be for a company to adopt an electric chair as its logo!) The reason they did so was because Jesus' death on a cross is the focal point of the Christian message.

The centrality of the cross to the Christian message was something established by Jesus Himself. Although He did many astonishing things and taught many profound truths, Jesus wanted to be remembered for His death. So, on the night before His death, He inaugurated the Lord's Supper; a meal that, among other things, pointed to His death. The broken bread would symbolise His body that would be broken in death, and the poured out wine would symbolise His blood that would be spilt in death (1 Corinthians 11:23-26).

Jesus' death, along with His resurrection, is foundational to Christian belief (1 Corinthians 15:3-5a). It is the centrepiece of God's plan of salvation (Luke 24:26-27). All that God did led up to the cross. It is the main emphasis of New Testament preaching (1 Corinthians 2:2). It is the leading theme of the worship in heaven (Revelation 5:12).

One of the clearest explanations of Jesus' death is found in Romans 3:21-26. In this passage, Paul invites us to accompany him on a tour of a 1st century town. He takes us to the courthouse, the market and the temple and uses what is going on at each place to help us get a handle on what was happening when Jesus died on the Hill of the Skull.

1. JESUS' DEATH SECURED FOR US A RIGHT RELATIONHSIP WITH GOD

We are taken into the courthouse to witness a trial, but to our horror we discover that it is our trial. We end up in the dock, and Paul, our tour guide, becomes the prosecuting lawyer. The charge against us is that we are unrighteous, that is, we have deliberately broken God's Law and as a result we are not in a right relationship with Him. In Romans 1:18-3:8, Paul presents the evidence against us. With ruthless and clinical efficiency, he analyses the lifestyle of three groups of people – the immoral materialist who only lives for himself, the person who is not religious but nevertheless lives a decent life, and the religious person who is up to his ears in spiritual stuff. Then, in Romans 3:9-20, Paul sums up his case. Without exception we are all guilty before God. "There is no one righteous" is the devastating conclusion to his penetrating investigation into our moral condition (Romans 3:10). We stand speechless in the dock (Romans 3:19), without a leg to stand on (Psalm 130:3). We are in deep, deep trouble, because if God condemned us without mercy, no one could accuse Him of being unfair (Psalm 51:4).

After the prosecuting lawyer has presented his case, everyone waits for God the Judge to pronounce His sentence. Surely there can be only one verdict – guilty as charged, but to our utter astonishment, God announces that we are not guilty. Gasps of amazement are heard around the courtroom. Has God taken leave of His senses? His Law condemns human judges who convict the innocent and let off the guilty (Proverbs 17:15). Does God have double standards? Here is God, issuing the legal judgment from the bench that the obviously guilty are not guilty.

Has He flipped? Doesn't He realise that the verdict He has just given is outrageous? The tabloids will have a field day. Then, after all the uproar has died down, God the Judge signals for Jesus to step forward. Pointing at Him, He says, "Here is the reason for the verdict I have just announced. I am able to pronounce these obviously guilty people "not guilty" on the basis of what Jesus achieved by His death on the cross".

Can God do anything? "Of course, He can," might be our immediate answer. However, it might surprise us to realise that this is not the answer the Bible gives. It states that God cannot do anything that contradicts His character (2 Timothy 2:13). If God is to bring us into a right relationship with Himself, He must do it in a way that is consistent with His character. God is inflexibly just and scrupulously fair, and cannot turn a blind eye to sin (Exodus 23:7 and 34:7). His justice demands that sin is punished. He will not condone sin in the slightest. However, God is also love (1 John 4:16). He does not take sadistic pleasure in seeing people punished for their sin. Instead He implores us to come to Him for forgiveness and life (Ezekiel 33:11), and acts to make sure that we do not experience His just judgment (John 3:16). In bringing us into a right relationship with Himself, God must act in a way that is consistent with His justice and His love. He cannot play one against the other. Our salvation is not a compromising trade-off between God's justice and love. He must satisfy His justice and simultaneously display His love. He must refuse to condone sin without principle and at the same time refuse to condemn sinners without mercy. God achieved this in Jesus' death.

❖ JESUS' DEATH – SATISFYING GOD'S JUSTICE

The demands of God's justice are clear: the person who sins must be punished with death (Ezekiel 18:20 and Romans 6:23). God's justice is inflexible; He does not tolerate sin and acts in judgment against those who sin. The breathtaking good news of the Christian message is that God has judged sin, not by punishing us, but by bearing the punishment Himself in the person of Jesus. On the cross Jesus acted as our substitute (1 Peter 3:18), suffering our death penalty (1 Peter 2:24). On the basis of Jesus dying in our place, God's uncompromising justice is satisfied. God's judgment has fallen, not on the sinner but on the sinner's substitute.

If there was one person who understood the meaning of Jesus dying in his place it was Barabbas, a Jewish terrorist. A thoroughly nasty piece of work, he had been captured by the Roman military authorities and sentenced to die by crucifixion. As he heard the guards unlocking the door of his cell on death row, he must have said to himself, "This is it". However, to his surprise he was told that he was free because someone else was going to be executed in his place.

The Jewish religious authorities wanted Jesus to be executed, but only Pilate, the Roman procurator of Judea, could sentence people to death, so they dragged Jesus in front of Pilate. After interrogating Him, Pilate wanted to let Jesus go. But the crowd, egged on by their leaders, were baying for His blood. In a last desperate attempt to get Jesus released, Pilate tried the Passover Amnesty. Each year, at the Jewish Feast of Passover, the Roman governor would release a notorious prisoner. It was a good public relations exercise, and besides Rome had plenty of prisoners, so the release of one was no big deal. Pilate decided to give the crowd the choice of Jesus or Barabbas. He was sure that they would choose Jesus, and so let him off the hook. But they opted for Barabbas, who was set free, while Jesus was crucified, literally dying in his place.

❖ JESUS' DEATH – DISPLAYING GOD'S LOVE.

The Bible describes God's love as unique. It is His own love, and this distinctive love of God is seen most clearly in Jesus' death (Romans 5:8). How does the cross show that God's love is in a league of its own? God gave *His Son*. In the person of Jesus, God gave Himself. He gave the very best. He could not have improved on His gift. He did not send us an impersonal message that described His love. Nor did He send a third party to tell about His love, but He came in person. More than that, God gave His Son *to die*. If Jesus had left the splendour of heaven and lived on earth just to set us an example, that would have been wonderful in itself, but Jesus was more than a role model. He was a Saviour, who died on the cross. Jesus gave Himself to the extreme – to a slow, horrible death by crucifixion and to the horror of being abandoned by His Father as He bore our sin. Yet there is even more to God's unique love. He gave His Son to die *for us*. From time to time we hear stories of heroic and brave people who sacrificed their lives for others (Romans 5:7). They usually make the supreme sacrifice for someone they love, or someone who is their friend, or someone who is important. God's love is distinctive because it was directed towards the unlovely and ugly. In Romans 5:6-10, Paul uses four unflattering terms – powerless, ungodly, sinners and enemies - to describe what we were like when Jesus died for us. We were spiritually impotent with nothing to offer God (Romans 5:6). We were thoroughly unattractive to God, the very opposite of what He was like (Romans 5:6). We were abject failures, who had completely blown it when it came to doing what God wanted us to do (Romans 5:8). We were openly hostile to God, wanting nothing to do with Him (Romans 5:10). Yet Jesus died for people like us.

Jesus' death as our substitute meant that God was able to declare the obviously guilty not guilty. Justice has been satisfied and love displayed. We have been forgiven.

The Bible uses several graphic word-pictures to describe how wonderful God's forgiveness is.

➤ God cancels the massive debt that we owe to Him but had no hope of ever paying off (Psalm 32:2).

➤ God totally decommissions our sin (Micah 7:19). That which is in the depths of the sea is irrecoverable.

➤ Often we turn our backs on some object we find

distasteful or disgusting. God puts our rebellion and failure, which He finds repulsive, out of sight (Isaiah 38:17).

➢ When He forgives us, God also forgets (Jeremiah 31:34). He will not dig up the past sometime in the future and hold our sins against us.

➢ God wipes the slate clean (Psalm 51:1). He gives us a brand new fresh start.

However we need more than forgiveness if we are to be in a right relationship with God. Psalm 15:1 asks the question: who can approach God? The rest of that psalm answers its own question by saying that only someone whose thoughts, motives, words and actions are 100% pure can approach God. Forgiveness only gives us a neutral status before God. It has removed our negative status before God, but it does not give us a positive status before Him. In order to be in a right relationship with God, we need to have lived a perfect life, which we have not done. However, if someone were to come and do it for us that would be a completely different ball game. The good news of the Christian message is that Jesus has done just that. Jesus' sinlessness kicks in at this point. When He acted as our substitute, He not only bore our punishment, He also kept God's Law perfectly for us. He not only died the death we should have died, He also lived the life we should have lived. On the cross, a great swap took place as God took our sin and transferred it to Jesus (2 Corinthians 5:21). God treated Jesus as He should have treated us, and punished Him for our sins (Isaiah 53:5-6), and then He took Jesus' perfect obedience and transferred it to us.

The theological term for all this is "imputation". Imagine that you are up to your ears in debt. Perhaps that is not too hard to imagine! You owe the bank thousands of pounds. There is no way you will ever pay it back. However, you have a friend who is a multi-millionaire. (I told you we were only using our imaginations.) If he went to your bank manager and wrote off your debts, that would be brilliant. However, you would still have nothing in your account. True, you would not have any minus signs in your bank statement, but if you checked your account balance at the ATM, it would read zero. Just suppose that your multi-millionaire friend went to your bank manager and said, "I want you to transfer everything in my account to my friend's account and you are to transfer everything in his account into mine". That would be absolutely fantastic. Not only would you be debt free, you would also be fabulously wealthy. That is what Jesus has done for you. God has imputed, or transferred, all your unrighteousness to Him and He has been punished for your unrighteousness. He has also imputed, or credited, all His righteousness to you, so that you have a perfection with which to approach God.

The term the Bible uses to describe what we have been looking at is "justification." It is not something God does in us, but is a legal declaration He makes about us. As Judge, He delivers a verdict that we are in a right relationship with Him because of what Jesus our substitute did. Our sins were imputed to Him, and His righteousness was imputed to us.

2. JESUS' DEATH SECURED OUR FREEDOM

On our tour of this 1st century town, Paul now escorts us out of the courthouse to the market. There were no out-of-town supermarkets in those days. Everything had to be bought in the market. Just like markets today, traders, selling all kinds of goods and food, tried to make their living wheeling and dealing. However, there was one commodity on sale in the 1st century market that you would not find in one today. Some people traded in buying and selling human slaves. Paul takes us straight to the slave market to explain something else that Jesus achieved when He died on the cross.

Slaves made up the largest segment of the population of the

Roman Empire in Paul's time. While some slaves were treated very badly, others were treated very humanely. Both groups held one thing in common – they were slaves, under someone else's control. A slave was a piece of property; not a "he" or a "she", but an "it". However, a slave could be set free if his family or friends paid his owner an agreed sum of money. The sum of money paid in order to secure the slave's freedom was called "the ransom," and this process of securing a slave's freedom by paying a ransom was known as "redemption".

The Bible uses that common occurrence to explain Jesus' death. Paul argues in Romans 1:18-3:20 that, not only is everyone guilty before God, but we are all under sin's control (Romans 3:9). Everyone is enslaved by destructive habits from which they cannot break free, no matter how hard they try. Every 1st January we resolve to stop doing something we have been doing for years. Every 2nd January we say to ourselves, "Here we go again," because we have broken our New Year's resolution. Our spiritual slavery stems from the fact that we were born to parents who were themselves slaves to sin (Psalm 51:5). We have also been conquered by sin, so in Psalm 19:13, David refers to how sin can rule over people. To cap it all, we are in debt to God because we have failed to keep His Law. In Matthew 6:12, Jesus refers to sin as being in debt. We need someone to come and redeem us because we have not got what it takes to pay the ransom that would secure our freedom. Jesus said that He would pay the ransom (Mark 10:45). The other New Testament writers underscore this, highlighting how Jesus' blood spilt in death would redeem us from sin's control (Romans 3:24, Ephesians 1:7 and 1 Peter 1:18-19). Jesus entered the slave market of our sin and secured our freedom at the cost of His death.

When he wrote about Jesus redeeming us, Paul also had in mind the Old Testament figure of the Kinsman-Redeemer. If a member of the family, for whatever reason, became a slave or faced the prospect of becoming a slave, it was the duty of the Kinsman-Redeemer to rescue that family member from slavery or the threat of slavery. You see the idea of the Kinsman-Redeemer being played out in various places in the Old Testament (Genesis 14:1-16 and Hosea 3:1-2), but especially in the book of Ruth. Naomi was in danger of losing the family property because of debts her husband had incurred. But Boaz acted as Kinsman-Redeemer and rescued Naomi from her predicament by paying the debts himself. No doubt the fact that he got Ruth, Naomi's widowed daughter-in-law, for his wife when he redeemed the land was an added incentive! The Old Testament figure of Kinsman-Redeemer pointed forward to Jesus. When God the Father saw the terrible plight of our slavery to sin, He asked, "Who will rescue My people from sin's control? Who will act as their Kinsman-Redeemer?" Then Jesus stepped forward and said, "Here I am. Send Me".

As a result of what Jesus has done, we are free from sin's control over our lives. However, we are not free to live as we please. Our new-found freedom is not a freedom to do our own thing, but a freedom to do what Jesus wants us to do (Galatians 5:13-14 and 1 Corinthians 6:19b-20). This might appear to be no freedom at all for it seems that we are simply exchanging one form of control for another. However, initial impressions are deceptive. When we are redeemed we do come under Jesus' control, but submitting to His control leads, not to enslavement, but to freedom. The paradox of the Christian life is that the more enthusiastically, actively and unreservedly we submit to Jesus' control over our lives, the more our lives are filled with joy, peace, satisfaction and wholeness (Mark 8:34-35).

3. JESUS' DEATH SECURED RENEWED FRIENDSHIP BETWEEN GOD AND US

The final stop on our tour of this 1st century town is the local temple. Paul uses what goes on there to give us a third angle on what was happening when Jesus died.

When we think about sin, our minds tend to focus mainly on how it affects us. The Bible has a completely different focal point, concentrating on how it affects God. The real tragedy of sin is not that it makes us feel bad, but that it makes God mad. He is not only angry at sin in general (Psalm 45:7), but He is also angry with those who commit sin (Psalm 5:5-6). His judgment hangs over them, ready to crash in on them (Ephesians 2:3a).

The idea that God is angry with sin and sinners – what is known as "the wrath of God" – infuriates some people.

➢ "God's wrath is contrary to His love," some protest. However, the Bible never sets these two aspects of God's character at each other's throat. They are allies, not opposites. The alternative to wrath is not love, but moral neutrality, and God is never morally neutral. He cannot tolerate sin in any shape or form (Habakkuk 1:13). He loves right living (Psalm 33:5) and applauds everything that is in line with His Word.

➢ "God's wrath is a slur on His character," others object. If God's anger is like human anger, then this objection does hold water. However, that is not how the Bible presents the idea of God's wrath. Human anger is often an inconsistent, uncontrollable and irrational rage. So often we simply lose it with others. We get all steamed up about nothing. Our anger is never free from being contaminated by jealousy, malice, animosity and a desire for revenge. In contrast, God's anger is absolutely free from all these poisonous ingredients. It is a consistent, rational antagonism towards sin that stems from His holiness. It is His revulsion at anything that is contrary to His holy character. It is His refusal to condone sin or to come to terms with it. He is actively hostile towards sin.

What is more, this hostility is not all one-way traffic. We are also hostile towards God (Romans 8:7). Instead of running to Him, we run away from Him, wanting nothing to do with Him. The end result of all this mutual animosity is alienation between God and us (Isaiah 59:2). If the friendship between God and us is to be restored, something has to be done about our sin.

When someone offends us, the normal scenario is that we wait for the other person to make the first move in sorting things out. "The ball is in her court," we say proudly. "If she wants to be friends with me again, she knows where I live." Even though He was the offended party, God took the initiative to restore the friendship between Himself and us (2 Corinthians 5:18 and 19). The healing of the relationship, which our sin had smashed into tiny bits, was God's work. He did so by means of Jesus' death.

Jesus' death pacified God's anger. The term the Bible uses is "propitiatory sacrifice" (Romans 3:25, 1 John 2:2 and 1 John 4:10). I know it is a bit of a mouthful, but it means that Jesus offered up His life as a sacrifice that would placate God's wrath. When He died, Jesus absorbed in His own innocent person the full fury of God's anger against our sin. The consequence of Jesus pacifying God's wrath is that the friendship between God and us has been restored (1 Peter 2:24-25 and 3:18).

Paul has finished his tour, but how do these three ideas of justification (the courthouse word-picture), redemption (the marketplace word-picture) and propitiation (the temple word-picture) fit together? James Boice in his book *The Foundations of the Christian Faith* explains their relationship using what he calls "The Salvation Triangle."

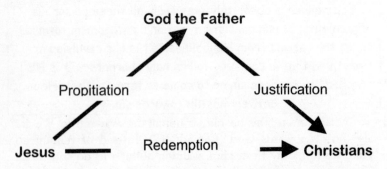

The arrow that points from God the Father to Christians indicates that justification is something God the Father has done for us. He has declared us "not guilty" and in a right relationship with Himself. The arrow that runs from Jesus to Christians signifies that redemption is something Jesus has done for us. He has set us free from sin's control. The arrow that goes from Jesus to God the Father points to how propitiation is something that Jesus did in relation to God the Father. By His death, He appeased, or propitiated, God's wrath against us and our sin, and, as a consequence, friendly relations between God and us are restored.

MAKING THE CONNECTION

How do we come to experience what Jesus achieved by His death? Even though the default setting in our lives is to try to earn God's salvation, the consequences of Jesus' death become contemporary in our lives only when we turn from our sins and believe in Jesus. Our best will never be good enough; we have to repent and have faith in Jesus (Galatians 3:11, Ephesians 2:9, Acts 3:19 and 16:31). Although the Bible makes clear that we cannot turn from our sins and trust in Jesus apart from God's activity in us (Acts 11:18 and Ephesians 2:8), it also says that repentance and faith involve us doing something. They are commands, and commands are things we must actively do and not things which are done for us.

Repentance is not feeling bad that our sin has made us unhappy or hurt others. It is being horrified that our sin has offended God and then making a deliberate decision to turn our back on it and to start to move towards Jesus. It is an about-turn as we stop doing our own thing and begin to go Jesus' way. We break off from all our attempts at a do-it-yourself salvation and start to look exclusively to Jesus to save us. Although repentance appears to be a negative, it is actually a positive. It is a no that is really a yes, because the minute we turn away from our sin, we discover that we have turned towards Jesus.

Faith is not a leap in the dark, done in some intellectual vacuum. It has content to it, because if it did not, it would just be superstition. We do not have to know everything about

Christianity in order to exercise faith, but there is a bottom line and it is grasping in our minds that we are sinners, and that Jesus has died for sinners. It means being attracted to Jesus because of what He has done. It also means actually placing our trust in Him, which is something, with God's help, that we must actually do. Faith is deliberately inviting Jesus to deal with our sin and take control of our lives (Revelation 3:20 and John 1:12). Faith is compared to eating food and drinking water (John 6:50-51 and John 4:10-14 and 7:37).

When we repent and believe in Jesus, all that He secured for us by His death becomes real and contemporary. We are put into a right relationship with God. We are set free from sin's control and brought under Jesus' gracious and kind rule. God is no longer angry with us and we are His friends. It is turning from our sins and placing our trust in Jesus that makes the connection between what Jesus achieved in the past and what we experience today.

DIGGING DEEPER

You might like to explore further some of the issues raised in this chapter by reading *The Cross He Bore* by Frederick Leahy (Published by Banner of Truth) and *The Message of the Cross* by Derek Tidball (Published by IVP).

7. RESTING IN PEACE OR RISEN IN POWER?

In this chapter, we are going to discover what the Bible says about Jesus' resurrection.

A REAL IN SPACE AND TIME EVENT
- **An historical event**
- **A physical event**

POINTERS TO THE RESURRECTION
- **Jesus' body was gone**
- **The not quite empty tomb**
- **Jesus was seen**
- **Lives were transformed**

A FOUNDATIONAL TRUTH
- **It backs up Jesus' claim to be God the Son**
- **It validates the achievements of Jesus' death**
- **It guarantees Jesus' gift of eternal life for us**
- **It assures us of Jesus' power**

In their book *What would Jesus say to...?* Steve Ayers and Jason Lane record the story of a conversation between two elderly women as they left church after witnessing something suspiciously modern in the service. They were not amused. One lady turned to her friend and declared, "It's enough to make Jesus turn in His grave". The Christian message is based upon the firm conviction that Jesus is not resting in peace in a grave in Israel, but that He is risen in power.

1. A REAL IN SPACE AND TIME EVENT

The death of someone close to us is devastating. After we have got over the initial shock, we try to rebuild our lives as best we can. It has been suggested that this is how Jesus' resurrection should be understood. It was the disciples getting their act together after the crushing blow of Jesus' death. It was Jesus' followers' morale that rose, not His body.

In the movie *Titanic* Rose (Kate Winslet's character) and Jack (Leonardo di Caprio's character) fall in love. Rose is rescued when the ship goes down, but Jack is drowned. At the end of the movie, when as an old woman Rose remembers her short romance with Jack, Celine Dion sings *My heart will go on*. In the song, Rose says that Jack is alive in her mind as the thought of those love-filled days still lives on in her memory. It has also been suggested that this is how Jesus' resurrection is to be thought of. After His death, Jesus lived on in His disciples' memory.

However, the Bible rejects both these explanations of Jesus' resurrection. In 1 Corinthians 15:3-5, Paul sets out the Bible's understanding of it.

❖ **AN HISTORICAL EVENT**

Jesus' resurrection can be pinpointed in history. It occurred "on the third day" by Jewish reckoning after His death (1 Corinthians 15:4). Jesus' resurrection happened in space and time, and not in the disciples' minds or hearts, being as much an historical fact as my birthday on 27th May 1955.

❖ **A PHYSICAL EVENT**

Died, buried, raised and appeared - the four verbs Paul uses in 1 Corinthians 15:3-5 - all relate to Jesus' physical body. It was Jesus' body that died and was buried, therefore, when he goes on to say that Jesus was raised and seen, Paul must be referring to the same physical body. It would be illogical for Paul to believe in a physical crucifixion and burial and then, mid-sentence and without flagging it up, suddenly switch to believing in a non-physical resurrection and appearances. Jesus' resurrection and appearances were as tangible as His death and burial. The same Jesus, who physically died and whose body was buried, was the same Jesus, who physically rose and whose body appeared to others.

When the Bible speaks about Jesus' resurrection, it means that He was physically and bodily raised from the dead in history.

2. POINTERS TO THE RESURRECTION

The Bible does not assert that Jesus rose from the dead without presenting us with evidence to back up its claim.

❖ JESUS' BODY WAS GONE

When the women arrived at Jesus' tomb on the first Easter Sunday morning, they discovered that the stone over the entrance to the tomb was rolled away and that Jesus' body had vanished (John 20:1-2). They went back to Jesus' disciples and told them what had happened. Peter and John went to investigate, and they found it just as the women had said (Luke 24:24). Jesus' body was no longer in the tomb. How do we explain its disappearance?

Women are sometimes accused of having a bad sense of direction. *Did the women go to the wrong tomb?* That is psychologically improbable. People do not forget where their loved ones are buried, and less than 48 hours before, these women had helped bury Jesus.

Did Jesus actually die on the cross? The suggestion was put around that Jesus only fainted on the cross. Then, in the coldness of the tomb, He revived, made His way back to the disciples and convinced them that He had conquered death. This explanation for the disappearance of Jesus' body just bristles with problems. For example, Pilate was convinced that Jesus was dead; otherwise he would not have given Joseph of Arimathea permission to remove Jesus' body from the cross. In fact, Pilate expressed surprise that Jesus had died so quickly (Mark 15:44). The Romans liked their victims to hang on crosses as long as possible, so that they could maximise the crowd-controlling potential of crucifixion. In death by crucifixion, the victim basically suffocated, so in order to speed up death, the victim's legs were broken. When the Roman execution squad came to Jesus, they did not break His legs because He was already dead (John 19:31-33). Just to double check, they thrust a spear into Jesus' side. These men who knew when a man was dead, were convinced that Jesus was dead. This idea that Jesus did not actually die on the cross is a non-runner.

Did the disciples steal Jesus' body? This was the spin the Jewish religious authorities used in order to explain away the fact that Jesus' body had gone AWOL. Again this explanation is seriously flawed. For a start, the disciples had no plans to stage-manage a resurrection. They should have known that Jesus would rise from the dead. On several occasions He had told them that He would (Matthew 16:21, Matthew 17:23, Matthew 20:19), and in several places the Old Testament predicted Jesus' resurrection (Psalm 16:10, Psalm 118:22-24, Job 19:25-27 and Isaiah 53:9-10). However, the disciples were slow out of the blocks when it came to grasping what Jesus was saying and what the Old Testament was teaching, so they were as much taken by surprise by Jesus' missing body as everyone else. They had no motive for stealing Jesus' body. The history of the first Christians records how they were imprisoned, flogged and even killed on account of their belief in and preaching about Jesus' resurrection. It is highly unlikely that they would have been prepared to preach about and suffer for something they knew to be a blatant lie.

Did the Jewish authorities impound Jesus' body? They were aware that Jesus had talked of rising from the dead and, in order to get their retaliation in first and avert any monkey business, they took the precaution of confiscating Jesus' corpse. There could be no resurrection if they had the body. This is the least likely explanation of why Jesus' body was gone. Within weeks of the resurrection, Jesus' disciples were on the streets preaching that Jesus was alive. All the authorities had to do in order to totally discredit the fledgling Jesus Movement was to produce the body. The fact that they did not seems to indicate that they had no body to produce.

The explanations for the disappearance of Jesus' body do not hold water. They lack any historical evidence to back them up. With the lack of any credible alternative, the best explanation of why Jesus' body was gone seems to be the one found in the Gospels. Jesus' body was gone because God had raised Him from the dead.

❖ THE NOT-QUITE EMPTY TOMB

When Jesus' lifeless body was prepared for burial, it was wrapped in strips of linen with spices placed in the folds (John 19:39-40). A separate cloth was wrapped around His head. He would have looked like a mummy, with only His face and neck bare. Then Jesus' bandaged corpse would have been placed up on a stone shelf within the tomb.

When Peter went into the tomb, he found that it was not quite empty. The grave clothes were still there. However, what was significant was the fact that the grave clothes were lying undisturbed as if Jesus' body had just passed through them. There was a gap between the strips of linen that covered Jesus' body and the head turban, where His neck and face had been (John 20:6-7). If Jesus' disciples had stolen the body or the authorities had impounded it, the grave clothes would not have been inside the tomb. If Jesus had only fainted and then recovered in the coldness of the tomb, the grave clothes would not have been left undisturbed. If He had discarded them before making His escape, they would have been scattered all over the place and not untouched. The most plausible explanation for the not quite empty tomb is that, when God raised Jesus from the dead, His new supernatural resurrection body just passed through the grave clothes, leaving them undisturbed.

John informs us that it was the fact of the undisturbed grave clothes that convinced him that Jesus was alive (John 20:8).

❖ JESUS WAS SEEN

It was Jesus' appearances after His resurrection that underlined its historical and bodily reality. In 1 Corinthians 15:3-5, Paul makes two parallel statements – Jesus died and was buried, and Jesus was raised and appeared. In the same way as Jesus' burial confirmed the reality of His death because we only bury dead people, so Jesus' appearances confirmed the reality of His resurrection.

Attempts have been made to cast doubt on the importance of these post-resurrection appearances by saying that they were merely hallucinations. However hallucinations usually have at least the following characteristics. They happen at the climax to a period of exaggerated wishful thinking, and the circumstances such as time, place and mood must be favourable. In the Bible's account of Jesus' appearances after His resurrection both these factors are absent.

There was no strong inward desire to see Jesus, as the disciples had no expectation that He would rise from the dead. Favourable outward circumstances were also missing. If these appearances had taken place in one or two places particularly associated with Jesus, and at the same time of the day – for example, when the light was bad – and to people who were especially fond of Jesus, then we would smell a rat. However, Jesus appeared in many different places (Matthew 28:16, Luke 24:13-35 and John 20:26), at different times of the day (Mark 16:9 and John 20:19), and to different types of people such as His brothers who did not believe in Him and Paul who hated Him (1 Corinthians 15:7-8). He appeared to people in a variety of moods, not just to Mary who was upset and crying (John 20:10-18) but also to Peter who was full of remorse (John 21:1-14 and 1 Corinthians 15:5) and to Thomas who was racked with doubts (John 20:24-29). He also appeared to groups of people (1 Corinthians 15:6). In the same way as politicians find it impossible to fool all of the people all of the time, so mass hallucination is extremely improbable.

It is difficult to explain these appearances as being merely hallucinations. The most plausible explanation of them is that they actually happened and that the risen Lord was seen.

❖ LIVES WERE TRANSFORMED

The radical change that took place in the disciples' lives is an important pointer to Jesus' resurrection. Mary's crushing sadness and sorrow was transformed into ecstatic joy (John 20:10-18). The disciples' paralysing fear was transformed into deep-seated peace (John 20:19-23). Thomas' sinful unbelief was transformed into rock-solid faith (John 20:24-29). Peter's dehabilitating weakness was transformed into dynamic power (John 21:15-19).

The pointers to Jesus' resurrection are clear. The only adequate explanation of these phenomena is the classic Christian affirmation that "the Lord is risen indeed".

> Some have correctly pointed out that there are differences in the Gospel accounts of Jesus' resurrection. For example, Matthew, Mark Luke and John all have a slightly different combination of women who went to the tomb on the first Easter Sunday. These differences are no reason for jumping to the conclusion that the first Christians invented the idea of Jesus rising from the dead. In fact, these differences actually give the various accounts a real feel. Stories that tie up too tightly make investigators suspicious of collusion and collaboration. Dave Burke in his book *Jesus Unplugged* uses this story to make that very point. In 1990 two English diamond merchants were robbed at gunpoint in their New York hotel room of gems worth £1.8 million. The NYPD were suspicious that the whole thing was a set up. What made the detectives uneasy was that there were no discrepancies in their stories. Both of them answered the detectives in the same way. The NYPD could not prove anything at the time. However, two years later an American was arrested for armed robbery in London, and he confessed to having staged the New York job. Both the diamonds and the robbery were fake, and it was a scam to defraud Lloyds of London of the insurance money. The detectives' suspicions turned out to be justified.
>
> If the disciples had got together to make up a resurrection story, I suspect that they would have taken care to eliminate any differences from their accounts. They would have wanted to convey the impression that everyone saw the same thing from exactly the same angle. That impression is missing from their accounts of Jesus'

resurrection. Their accounts have the feel of eyewitness reports of actual events. The differences actually serve to highlight the honesty of Matthew, Mark, Luke and John.

3. A FOUNDATIONAL TRUTH

Jesus' death and resurrection are the twin pillars upon which the Christian message rests (1 Corinthians 15:1-5). Why is Jesus' resurrection as an in space and time fact so crucial?

❖ **IT BACKS UP JESUS' CLAIM TO BE GOD THE SON**

Slowly but surely the disciples caught on to Jesus' direct and indirect claims to be God. When Jesus was executed, their hopes and dreams were smashed into a million pieces (Luke 24:19-21). His claim to be God and His death on the cross did not fit together. Then God raised Jesus from the dead to openly declare that He was who He claimed to be (Romans 1:4).

❖ **IT VALIDATES THE ACHIEVEMENT OF JESUS' DEATH**

Jesus often predicted that His death would be different from every other death. He asserted that His death would secure His people salvation (Matthew 20:28). Did it achieve what He said it would achieve? Jesus' resurrection shows that God did accept Jesus' death as a sacrifice for sin. The Bible states that Jesus' death guarantees for us a right relationship with God, secures our freedom from sin's stranglehold on our lives, and brings about our friendship with God (Romans 4:24-25, 1 Peter 1:18-19 and 1 Peter 3:18). Jesus' resurrection was God's stamp of approval on all that Jesus had achieved as He died on the cross. In 1 Corinthians 15:13-20, Paul forces us to think the unthinkable: what if Jesus had not been raised from the dead? One of the dire consequences would be that our sins have not been forgiven (1 Corinthians 15:17). God would not have accepted Jesus' death as the only way of dealing radically and effectively with our sins. But Jesus has been raised from the dead (1 Corinthians 15:20), so our forgiveness is certain.

❖ **IT GUARANTEES JESUS' GIFT OF ETERNAL LIFE TO US**

If sex was the taboo subject for the Victorians, death is a no no for us. If you want to be a party pooper, then raise the issue of death the next time you are invited out for a meal. However, death is the only thing we can be certain about in life with the ultimate statistic being that one out of one dies. Jesus' resurrection assures us that death does not have the last word in our lives. The Bible portrays death as a warrior and a scorpion, but the warrior has been defeated and the scorpion has had its lethal sting pulled by Jesus' resurrection (1 Corinthians 15:55). Jesus guarantees everyone who believes in Him that they too will share in His victory over death (1 Corinthians 15:58).

❖ **IT ASSURES US OF JESUS' POWER.**

Our society is becoming increasingly self-obsessed. How can we be different and function outside the narrow confines of looking after Number One? The only way in which we can live outside society's box is in Jesus' resurrection power. God has promised that the very power He exerted in raising Jesus from the dead is available to us (Ephesians 1:19-20a). That is breathtakingly staggering! We are conscious of our failure to be different from others. Selfishness leaves its muddy footprints over all of our actions, even our best ones, but God has promised us resurrection power in order that we might live for Jesus and point people away from ourselves to Him.

The kids in our church youth club introduced me to the music of a band called 'The Offspring'. Apart from the raw energy of their music, what struck me was the bleak hopelessness of their lyrics. Their song *The kids Aren't Alright* reflect the profound pessimism that permeates our society. However, the message of Jesus' resurrection generates hope.

It causes Christians to be hopeful about the past. Our sins have been effectively dealt with and forgiven. Jesus' resurrection guarantees that. It produces hope for the present. We are not doomed to be like everyone else and live inside the box of self-centredness. We have power to be different and live for Jesus and His glory. It makes Christians hopeful about the future. One day our bodies will be resurrected, as Jesus' body was, and we will be raised to a new level of life in heaven.

In a world of hopelessness, the Christian message that Jesus is alive really is good news! Let's not keep it to ourselves.

DIGGING DEEPER

You might like to explore further some of the issues raised in this chapter by reading *The Day Death Died* by Michael Green (Published by IVP) and *The Message of the Resurrection* by Paul Beasley-Murray (Published by IVP).

8. THE END GAME

> **In this chapter, we are going to discover what the Bible says about Jesus' return.**
> **JESUS WILL RETURN AGAIN**
> **JESUS WILL RETURN AGAIN IN A SPECIFIC WAY**
> - **A historical event**
>   - **Personal**
>   - **Glorious**
>   - **Unexpected**
>   - **Signalled**
>
> **JESUS WILL RETURN AGAIN FOR A PURPOSE**
> - **To save His people**
> - **To punish His enemies**
>
> **JESUS WILL RETURN AGAIN, SO BE READY.**
> - **We are to work hard in Jesus' service**
> - **We are to be pure in our life style**
> - **We are to be steady under pressure**

I know that this may confirm your suspicions about me, but my initial career choice was to be a history teacher. When I told a friend this, she looked horrified. "Oh, no!" she gasped, "Can't you think of anything else? History's so boring." She would have agreed with Henry Ford's statement during his libel case against the *Chicago Tribune* in July 1919, that "History is bunk". I think she had been scarred for life by having to learn the order and dates of 18th and 19th century British Prime Ministers.

The Bible does not share this opinion of history. History is important to God as it is the arena in which He works out His masterplan for the world. To use the old cliché, history is His story. He began history with the creation. He brought history to its defining phase with Jesus' birth, life, death, resurrection and ascension. One day, He will bring history to a climactic end with Jesus' return to earth for a second and final time. History is not cyclical, repeating itself as it goes around in circles, but linear, moving in a straight line towards a terminal point – Jesus' return.

His Second Coming is the final play in history's end game.

Christians sometimes shy away from thinking about Jesus' Second Coming because it has often been highjacked by the lunatic fringe of the church. We are embarrassed to talk about it in case we are labelled cranks. This should not be so. The thought of Jesus' return thrilled the first Christians. There are over 300 references to it in the New Testament – on average, one every thirteen verses! The truth that one day the end game of history will be played out when Jesus returns to earth is as much part and parcel of the Christian message as Jesus' birth, life, death and resurrection. It ought to play a greater part in our thinking than it presently does. We should be like Lord Shaftesbury, the great British 19th century social reformer, who, near the end of his life, said, "I do not think that in the last forty years I have lived one conscious hour that was not influenced by the thought of our Lord's return".

1. JESUS WILL RETURN AGAIN

The Bible described Jesus' return as "the blessed hope" (Titus 2:13). When it uses that description of Jesus' return, we need to realise that it does not use the word "hope" in the same way as we do. For us, the word "hope" carries with it a good deal of uncertainty. For example, during the summer you are planning to invite your friends round for a barbeque. "I hope it does not rain," you think to yourself, yet you have a sneaking suspicion that it will. Our use of the word "hope" carries with it the baggage of uncertainty. The New Testament uses the word in exactly the opposite way. The word "hope" carries with it the idea of certainty. So when it calls Jesus' return "the blessed hope," it is indicating that there are no "ifs" and "buts" about it taking place. It definitely will happen.

Jesus Himself said that He would come back (John 14:3, Matthew 24:27 and 30, Matthew 25:31 and Mark 14:62). Angels called attention to it when they spoke to the disciples on the Mount of Olives after Jesus went back into heaven (Acts 1:9-12). It is referred to frequently in the New Testament letters

101

(Philippians 3:20, 1 Thessalonians 4:15-16, 2 Thessalonians 1:7-10, Titus 2:13 and Hebrews 9:23).

The certainty of Jesus' return is the bedrock to our hope for the future. However, its truth has been questioned.
➢ It has been challenged because it has been so long in taking place. This is not a new objection to the Second Coming (2 Peter 3:3-4). People argue that the first Christians expected Jesus to return in their lifetime. Not only did that not happen, but also nearly 2000 years have passed and still Jesus has not come back. If the first Christians got it wrong about the time of Jesus' return, these people say, then they were probably mistaken about the fact of Jesus' return as well. However, the sceptic's argument is flawed because the New Testament writers did not get it wrong about the time of Jesus' return. None of them categorically stated that Jesus would come back in their lifetime. In fact, Jesus Himself did not know the precise time of His return (Mark 13:32) and warned His followers about speculating about when He would come back (Acts 1:7). If the first Christians did not get it wrong as to the time of Jesus' return, then, to use the sceptics' own line of reasoning against them, they were not mistaken about the fact of His return either.
➢ A member of my congregation was told he would have heart surgery as soon as a cardiac intensive care bed became available. He knew that he was definitely going to have a by-pass operation but he was not exactly sure when. So he began to live, in his words, "as if I was going to have my operation within the next hour". He packed a bag and kept it beside the front door. He kept his mobile phone switched on all the time. He lived like that for two weeks,

102

and when the phone call came he was able to drop
everything and get to the hospital immediately. If we know
that something is definitely going to happen in the future
but we are not exactly sure when it will actually happen, we
have to live as if it could happen at any moment. The first
Christians were certain about the fact of Jesus' return but
uncertain about its timing. This is why they lived as if Jesus
could come back at any moment.

➢ Jesus' return has also been questioned because people
want to be able to live as they please. Unless there is a
Judgment Day and a perfect Judge to whom we are
accountable, we will live as we please. For example, at school
most of us tried to do as little as possible. The only thing
that motivated us to work was the exam at the end of the
year and a teacher who would not be best pleased if we did
not produce the goods in the exam. The idea of judgment
has a regulating effect on people's behavior. If there is no
Judgment Day and no perfect Judge, then we can live as we
like for there is no one to call us to account. This is why
people deny the fact of Jesus' return. They want to justify
the way they live.

2. JESUS WILL RETURN AGAIN IN A SPECIFIC WAY

Jesus' return will be a unique event. We get a flavour of its
extraordinary nature from passages such as Matthew 24:27 and
30-31 and 1 Thessalonians 4:16-17. The Second Coming is
something beyond our experience and even our imagination. For
example, we find it impossible to get our heads around how the
inhabitants of both hemispheres will see Jesus simultaneously
(Revelation 1:7).

❖ JESUS' RETURN WILL BE A HISTORICAL EVENT

In 1 Thessalonians 4:13-18, Paul tackles the sensitive issue of death by reminding these grieving Christians of the implications of Jesus' death, resurrection and return. Jesus' death and resurrection were both space and time events. By linking the Second Coming to them, Paul is saying that Jesus' return will be as literal and historical as these events.

❖ JESUS' RETURN WILL BE PERSONAL

Jesus Himself – not a deputy or a representative – will come again (1 Thessalonians 4:16). The same Jesus, who appeared on the stage of history at His birth and who then disappeared from the stage of history when He ascended into heaven after His death and resurrection, will reappear on the stage of history for a second and final time. A Greek word used in connection with Jesus' return is "parousia". It points to the presence of a member of the royal family in town for an official visit. When Jesus returns, He will be physically present once more on the earth.

❖ JESUS' RETURN WILL BE GLORIOUS

The first time He was on earth Jesus came in anonymity and humility. He appeared incognito, as the great Nobody in an out-of-the-way corner of an obscure part of the Roman Empire. Hardly anyone apart from a few shepherds and a couple of senior citizens realised He had come. It will be a different ball game when He returns. Jesus will come back in all His magnificent splendour as "the King of kings and Lord of lords" (Revelation 19:16). Another Greek word used in connection with Jesus' return is "apocalypse," which means "an unveiling", and conjures up the picture of someone opening the curtains on a beautiful summer's morning to reveal the brightness of the sun. When He came the first time, Jesus' glory was hidden, and people did not recognise Him for who He was. When He returns, the curtain will be pulled wide open and Jesus' glory will be unveiled for everyone to see. He will return in the glory that Peter, James and John glimpsed when Jesus was transfigured (Mark 9:2-3). He will come back in the splendour with which Isaiah saw Him in the Temple (Isaiah 6:1-5). He will appear again with all the outward

104

trappings of His divine status that He set to one side when He came the first time (1 Thessalonians 4:16-17 and 2 Thessalonians 1:7b). It will be an occasion of unparalleled magnificence.

---

1 Thessalonians 4:16-17 presents Jesus as God the Son who has conquered all His enemies.

➤ The trumpet blast is a reminder that God Himself was about to appear (Exodus 19:16-17 and Isaiah 27:13)

➤ The clouds signify God's presence (Exodus 19:9, Daniel 7:13 and Matthew 24:30).

➤ Christians will go up to meet Jesus in the air and immediately accompany Him to earth, just as in the ancient world citizens of a city ran out to meet their king when he returned victorious from battle and escorted him back into the city (1 Samuel 18:6 and Psalm 24:7-10).

Jesus will return as the mighty conqueror in an open and public display of His glory and splendour.

❖ JESUS' RETURN WILL BE UNEXPECTED

When it comes to highlighting the unexpected nature of Jesus' return, the Bible uses two metaphors.

• The picture of a thief coming to rob a house (Matthew 24:43-44 and 1 Thessalonians 5:2). If you have ever had the dreadful experience of having your house burgled, you will know how surprised you were. "This sort of things happens to other people," a friend of mine said to me after his house had been broken into, "but I never expected it to happen to me!" No burglar will send you an e-mail asking you to be out on a certain night because he wants to rob you. He will just do it unannounced.

• The picture of a woman going into labour (Matthew 24:8 and 1 Thessalonians 5:3). A pregnant woman might know that she will go into labour, but when she actually does, she is often taken by surprise.

❖ JESUS' RETURN WILL BE SIGNALLED

The counter balance to the Bible's teaching about the unexpectedness of the Second Coming is the New Testament data that certain things must happen before Jesus' returns.

- The good news about Jesus will spread worldwide (Matthew 24:14), so that heaven will be populated by a huge gathering from every people-group on earth (Revelation 7:9).

- Ethnic Israel's rejection of Jesus will come to an end and large numbers of Jewish people will become Christians (Romans 11:25-29).

- People will turn their backs on the Christian faith and those who remained loyal to Jesus will face severe pressure, opposition and persecution (Matthew 24:12, 2 Thessalonians 2:3, 1 Timothy 4:1 and Revelation 7:13-14).

- A figure whom Paul calls "the Man of Lawlessness" will make an appearance (2 Thessalonians 2:3-12). Although an anti-Christian spirit has always existed (1 John 4:3) and many people who have been openly hostile to Christianity have strutted their stuff on the stage of history (1 John 2:18), Paul leads us to expect that just before Jesus returns an individual who will be the embodiment of evil will arrive on the scene to lead a great final assault on God, His people and all that is good.

The Bible specifies that, in the run-up to Jesus' return, two things will be happening in parallel – Jesus' Kingdom will make great advances with both Jews and non-Jews becoming His followers, and Satan's kingdom will retaliate with frantic ferocity.

Revelation 20:4 speaks of Jesus reigning for 1000 years. The Latin word for "thousand" is "mille," from which we get our word "millennium". One of the great points of controversy among Christians is the relationship of Jesus' return to the Millennium.

> ➤ Christians who are *Premillennialist* believe that Jesus will come back before the Millennium. (The prefix "pre" means "before".) His return will usher in a literal one thousand year reign from Jerusalem that will be characterised by political peace, economic prosperity and the Jews being given a prominent position.

> ➤ Christians who are *Postmillennialist* believe that Jesus will come back after the Millennium. (The prefix "post" means "after".) Before Jesus returns the church will experience a golden age of spiritual prosperity. The gospel will make a huge impact with an increasingly large proportion of the world's inhabitants becoming Christians. Not everyone will become a Christian nor will sin be totally eliminated, but the world will experience an unprecedented spiritual renewal.

> ➤ Christians who are *Amillennialist* reject a literal interpretation of the Millennium. (The prefix "a" indicates a negative.) The 1000 years symbolizes Jesus' present spiritual rule over all which began with His ascension (Philippians 2:9-11 and Psalm 2:6-9), and is actually a description of world history between Jesus' two comings. None of these views of the Millennium of Revelation 20:4 is without its difficulties. We need to run with the one with the least problems.

3. JESUS WILL RETURN AGAIN FOR A PURPOSE

The Bible is unanimous that the purpose of Jesus' return is to judge (Psalm 9:8 and 96:10, Matthew 25:31-32a, John 5:27-30, Acts 17:31, Romans 14:10 and 2 Corinthians 5:10). The idea behind the concept of judging is that of dividing, and the crucial number is two.

On Judgment Day, Jesus will divide all humanity into two different groups – those who have rejected the gospel and refused to believe in Him as their Saviour and Lord, and those who have accepted the gospel and trusted in Him as their Saviour and Lord. In the stories He told about judgment, Jesus spoke about a shepherd who separated the sheep from the goats in his flock (Matthew 25:31-33), a fisherman who sorted the good fish from the bad ones in his catch (Matthew 13:47-50), and harvesters who divided the wheat from the weeds in their crop (Matthew 13:24-30 and 36-43).

Jesus will pronounce one of two verdicts on everyone. Those who have rejected Jesus will receive a verdict of condemnation (Matthew 25:41). Those who have welcomed Jesus into their lives will receive a verdict of salvation (Matthew 25:34).

After Judgment Day, people will go to one of two destinations. Heaven will be the place to which Jesus' followers will go. Those who have refused to believe in Him will end up in hell.

The Old Testament prophets spoke about something called "the Day of the Lord." It would a time when God would decisively intervene in history in order to act against His enemies and to rescue His people (Joel 3:14-21 and Obadiah 15-21). In the New Testament this motif was applied to Jesus' return (1 Thessalonians 5:2, 2 Thessalonians 2:2 and 2 Peter 3:10). They realised that all the other days of the Lord that had occurred in history pointed to the great Day of the Lord when Jesus would come back. When Jesus returns He will do what God promised He would do on the Day of the Lord. He will judge the nations by saving His people and punishing His enemies (1 Thessalonians 5:9 and 2 Thessalonians 1:8-9).

❖ JESUS WILL SAVE HIS PEOPLE

The Bible presents Jesus' salvation as a three dimensional thing. The past phase focused on how, on the basis of His death, Jesus saved us from sin's penalty and guilt. The present element has to do with how, through the activity of His Holy Spirit, Jesus saves us from sin's power. The future aspect centres on how Jesus will save us from sin's presence in our lives. He will do this by giving us new resurrection bodies like His. The Christian's body is the frontline in the battle against sin (Romans 6:12-13). We are to show our commitment to Jesus through our eyes, mouths, feet, hands and ears. Sadly we discover that our present bodies are poor tools for expressing our longing to obey God. Our residual sinful natures entice us into sin. We become a puzzle to ourselves (Romans 7:14-25). Part of the Christian's hope is that, when He returns, Jesus will give us new resurrection bodies freed from sin (1 Corinthians 15:51-57). For those who like theo-speak, the word is "glorification." The work of salvation will be completed in us, with every tendency to turn our backs on God finally abolished. We will be liberated from all our self-centredness, and God's image in us will be perfectly restored. We will be sinless creatures in bodies uncontaminated by sin, the ideal vehicle through which to worship, serve and know God throughout eternity.

WELCOME HOME.

What is heaven like? The Bible describes it as a city (Hebrews 11:10) and a country (Hebrews 11:16). My favourite is the picture of heaven as a home (John 14:2).

➤ Heaven is a place of glory. It is the "Father's house," and our Father is the God of awesome glory (Exodus 15:11). When he wrote down his glimpse into heaven in the book of Revelation, John wrote in symbols and picture-language. God's glory was so overwhelming that he found ordinary language and figures of speech hopelessly inadequate to describe what heaven and the God of heaven is like.

➤ Heaven is a place of meeting. Heaven is where Jesus is (John 14:3) for right at the centre of heaven is a throne upon which He sits (Revelation 4 and 5). In heaven we will meet Jesus, and we will perfectly enjoy seeing and being with Him.

➤ Heaven is a place of reunion. God's family will be

109

reunited in heaven. Not only will we be reunited with Jesus, our Elder Brother, but also with other Christians down through the centuries, our spiritual sisters and brothers. We will meet up with them, not in some vague way, but in the deepest possible way – the worship of God and Jesus (Revelation 5:11-14).

➤ Heaven is a place of rest. Our daily life-or-death combat with sin will be finished. The long war will be over.

➤ We must not imagine that in heaven we will sit around twiddling our thumbs, because it is a place of activity. We will worship and serve God from hearts that have been set perfectly free to love. Unimpeded by sin, we will be able to pursue our great desire of getting to know our God and Saviour more and more.

➤ Heaven is a place of belonging. When I started my first job, I lived with a family as a lodger. The family were extremely kind, but it was their home and not mine. Then I got a place of my own. It was home. Christians are temporary residents on earth (1 Peter 2:11). Beautiful as the world can be and good as life can sometimes be, we do not really belong here. Our true home is in heaven (Philippians 3:20). In heaven, Jesus has prepared a place just for us (John 14:2-3). We will belong there. We will be home at last.

❖ **JESUS WILL PUNISH HIS ENEMIES**

Jesus will "take vengeance" on His enemies (2 Thessalonians 1:8). In Jesus' vengeance, there are none of the evils that characterise human revenge – no malice, no personal vindictiveness and no gloating over the victim's misfortune. Jesus' punishment is judicial. He will be acting like a judge, passing sentence in line with the standards of His law. His judgment will be just, legal, fair and totally above board.

> The idea of judicial vengeance or retributive punishment is foreign to people's thinking today. If the idea of punishment is entertained at all, it is only in terms of punishment that reforms the offender or deters others from copying the offender's behaviour. They cannot get their heads around the thought of judicial vengeance. The Bible, however, sees punishment mainly in terms of retribution, with the cross being the great example. Jesus did not die as a deterrent, nor so that He could be reformed. His death was a judicial act of retributive punishment on God's part as He bore the punishment that should have been handed down to us because of our sin.

Jesus will punish those who have refused to trust in Him as their Saviour and follow Him as their Lord (2 Thessalonians 1:8). Their punishment will be self-chosen. They will have brought it upon themselves by deliberately loving darkness rather than light, consciously choosing not to have their Creator as their Lord, calculatingly preferring self-indulgent sin to self-denying obedience to Jesus, and purposely rejecting Jesus rather than coming to Him (John 3:18-21, Romans 1:18, 24, 26, 28 and 32, Romans 2:8 and 2 Thessalonians 2:9). When Jesus acts against them in judgment, they will have no one to blame but themselves.

The punishment of those who refuse to trust in Jesus is hell. The Bible describes hell as a place of fire and darkness (Jude 7 and 13), of weeping (Matthew 8:12), of destruction (2 Peter 3:7) and of torment (Revelation 20:10). It is a place of total distress and misery. It is a place where God's anger is not diluted with His mercy. I spoke to a man who had fought in World War II. He was in action at D-Day. He was among the first to liberate the Belsen concentration camp. He had experienced the raw horror of war. "It was hell on earth," he told me. Terrible as his experiences undoubtedly were, God had been good to him. He returned from the war alive, and had known the camaraderie of his pals. In hell, there is no goodness, kindness, love, joy or mercy; only God's just anger expressed in all its fury. Hell on earth has only occurred once in history, and that was when the Father turned His back on Jesus as He died for our sins. When Jesus screamed out, "My God, My God, why have You abandoned Me?" that, and that alone, was hell on earth. The Bible sees this punishment in hell as unending (Jude 13 and Revelation 20:10). Popular ideas about people getting a second chance after death, or the personal annihilation of the wicked at some stage, are not supported by the biblical data.

4. JESUS WILL RETURN AGAIN, SO BE READY

A friend leads a small Bible study in his home for new Christians and people interested in finding out more about Jesus. He told me that the chat after the study nearly always focuses on Jesus' return. People are fascinated by it. However, the Bible's teaching about the Second Coming is designed to challenge us to action and not to tickle our minds. We live in-between Jesus' two comings. How then should we live?

❖ **WE ARE TO WORK HARD IN JESUS' SERVICE**

Jesus gave us work to do while He is away. He expects us to get on with that work (Luke 12:42-43). We are to work hard at living for Jesus in our homes and the places where we work, study and relax. We are to be busy trying to help people who are in need. This will be one of the criteria Jesus uses to evaluate our lives when He judges us (Matthew 25:31-46). We are to be active in getting the good news about Jesus out to others. Jesus' final instructions to His people were that we should take the good news to every place on earth (Matthew 28:18-20, Luke 24:45-51 and Acts 1:8-9). Those instructions have never been withdrawn or modified. Each Christian has a responsibility to carry out this work. Jesus' absence is not an excuse for idleness. It is the reverse. It is an incentive to work hard in Jesus' service, so that, on Judgment Day, we will hear Him say those glorious words: "Well done, good and faithful servant" (Matthew 25:21 and 23).

❖ WE ARE TO BE PURE IN OUR LIFE STYLE

This is a recurring theme in the New Testament (Titus 2:11-14, 2 Peter 3:11-12 and 14, and 1 John 3:3). When we were at school, we all had the experience of doing something naughty and being caught out by the teacher's sudden return to the classroom. We do not want to be caught out by Jesus' return. We want to be living a consistently pure life so that we will not be ashamed at His coming (1 John 2:28). We are to stop filth from building up in our lives. We are to refuse to become preoccupied with trivialities. We are not to ignore anything, even seemingly small matters, that might short-circuit our fellowship with God. We are to regularly come to Jesus and ask Him to deal with our sin (1 John 1:9).

❖ WE ARE TO BE STEADY UNDER PRESSURE

On numerous occasions, Jesus warned us to expect opposition (John 15:19 and John 16:33). Paul ran with this strand of teaching in many of his letters (Acts 14:22 and 2 Timothy 3:12). Pressure, trouble, difficulties, hostility, abuse, slander and persecution are all par for the course in the Christian life. We are to be steady when we are under pressure (Revelation 2:25). How? Because we know that Jesus is coming back. On that day He will right all the wrongs done against us and He will reward us for being His servants in a hostile world.

John Wesley, the founder of Methodism, was asked if he would make any adjustments to his life if he knew that Jesus was coming back the next day. Wesley's answer was short and to the point: "No!" He was ready for Jesus' return.

DIGGING DEEPER

You might like to explore further some of the issues raised in this chapter by reading *A Window on Tomorrow* by Liam Goligher (Published by Christian Focus Publications), *The Message of Thessalonians* by John Stott (Published by IVP as part of *The Bible Speaks* Today series) and *Revelation Unwrapped* by John Richardson (Published by St Matthias Press).

9. WE ARE NOT ALONE

> **In this chapter, we are going to discover what the Bible says about the Holy Spirit.**
> **WHO ARE YOU, HOLY SPIRIT?**
> - **The Holy Spirit is a person**
> - **The Holy Spirit is God**
>
> **WHAT DO YOU DO, HOLY SPIRIT?**
> **He glorifies Jesus**
> - **By bringing us to Jesus**
> - **By reassuring us that we belong to Jesus**
> - **By teaching us about Jesus**
> - **By creating and nurturing in us a love for Jesus**
> - **By making us more like Jesus**
> - **By helping us to live for Jesus**
> - **By enabling us to serve Jesus**
> - **By empowering us in our witness to Jesus**

The first time we meet someone, somewhere in that initial conversation we will ask two questions: who are you and what do you do? Perhaps you reckon that we do not need to ask these two questions about the Holy Spirit because He is hardly a total stranger to most Christians today. However, there is still a fair bit of woolly thinking knocking around in connection with who He is and what He does. So perhaps we do need to revisit these two basic questions.

1. WHO ARE YOU, HOLY SPIRIT?
❖ THE HOLY SPIRIT IS A PERSON

He is not some impersonal force à la *Star Wars*, but a person; not an "it" but a "He". He has a mind with which He knows (1 Corinthians 2:10-12), emotions with which He feels because He can be insulted and disappointed (Ephesians 4:30), and He has a will with which He acts (Acts 16:6). Knowing, feeling and acting are the three components that go to make up what we call "personality". The Holy Spirit can be sinned against (Matthew 12:31-32), and we do not sin against an impersonal influence.

❖ THE HOLY SPIRIT IS GOD

Not only did the apostles, whose minds were saturated with the Old Testament conviction that God is one, come to see that Jesus was God, they also realised that the Holy Spirit was God. Acts 5:1-11 records the story of how Ananias and Sapphira, a husband and wife, tried to trick the first Christians into thinking that they were more spiritual than they actually were. Peter, acting as the spokesman for the apostles, confronts them. He accuses them of lying to the Holy Spirit (Acts 5:3), and then, in the next breath, accuses them of lying to God (Acts 5:4). In Peter's mind, the Holy Spirit was God, so lying to Him was the same as lying to God.

The Bible's twin-track answer to the question "Who are You, Holy Spirit?" is straightforward. He is a divine person, distinct from but equal with the Father and the Son.

2. WHAT DO YOU DO, HOLY SPIRIT?

Jesus gives us a simple but profound answer to that question at the start of John 16:14. The Spirit's role is to glorify Jesus by directing our attention to Him. He never wants to be centre stage; instead everything He does is designed to promote Jesus' reputation. How does He do that?

❖ BY BRINGING US TO JESUS

We cannot become Christians apart from the Holy Spirit's activity (John 3:5) because only He has the power to overcome the double problem of our unwillingness and inability to trust in Jesus.

We do not want to follow Jesus because we see that as restricting our freedom and cramping our style. We enjoy our independence from God. We do not see ourselves as being in a perilous spiritual position (Romans 1:18 and Ephesians 2:1-3). What the Holy Spirit does is to act like a prosecuting lawyer and drive home to our minds and consciences the seriousness of sin, our need for Jesus' forgiveness and the certainty of standing before God on Judgment Day and being condemned to hell because of our rebellion against Him (John 16:9-11). The theological term for what the Holy Spirit does is known as "conviction of sin". When this happens, our easy-going attitude to sin and judgment vanishes, and we now want to trust in Jesus because we see Him no longer as an irrelevancy, but as our only hope of salvation.

However, although we might want to trust in Jesus, we do not have the ability to do so. What the Holy Spirit does is to give us the faith and repentance needed to turn from our sins and to trust in Jesus. This was one of God's promises of salvation (Jeremiah 31:33 and Ezekiel 36:26-27). The Holy Spirit transforms our inward disposition – the term the Bible uses is "the heart". He changes our hostility towards God into a love for God and our love of sin into a hostility towards sin. The theological term for this internal revolution is known as "regeneration". Once the Holy Spirit has regenerated our hearts, we have the ability to trust in Jesus.

The Holy Spirit normally uses God's Word to bring about conviction of sin and regeneration (Acts 2:37, Acts 16:14 and 1 Peter 1:23-25). This is why it is vital that in our evangelism we are constantly trying to bring people into contact with the Bible. We will not only pray that our friends will become Christians, we will also ask them along to church to hear God's Word being preached, or invite them along to a Bible study, or get them to start reading the Bible for themselves. When we expose people to the Bible, the Holy Spirit uses the Word He inspired to unfog their minds so that they can see where they really stand in relation to God and also to change their wills so that they come to the place where they put their trust in Jesus.

❖ BY REASSURING US THAT WE BELONG TO JESUS

Although we can lack assurance of salvation and still be in a right relationship with Him (1 John 5:13), God wants us to have a joyful yet humble confidence that we are Christians. This is something that Christians down through the centuries have experienced (Job 19:25-27, Psalm 73:23-24, Romans 8:38-39 and 2 Timothy 1:12). This reassurance that we are Christians comes as a result of the Holy Spirit's activity in our lives (Romans 8:14-16).

How can we be sure that the Holy Spirit lives within us? Our lifestyle answers that question. Although we are saved by faith alone, saving faith is never alone. The Holy Spirit's presence will be seen in the way we live. 1 John outlines three evidences of the Spirit's presence in us: a new obedience to God's Word (1 John 2:3), a new love for other Christians (1 John 3:14) and a new delight in the truth (1 John 5:1). God does not ask if we obey His Word perfectly, if we have a perfect love for other Christians, or if we take a perfect delight in the truth. He is not looking for perfection. He simply asks you if these evidences of the Spirit's presence are there at all. We may not be what we ought or would like to be, but, if we can honestly say that we are not what we used to be, that is fine with God.

In Ephesians 1:13-14, Paul describes the Holy Spirit as a seal. A seal is a mark of ownership, like the brand a rancher would burn on to the hide of his cattle to distinguish them from another rancher's cattle. The Holy Spirit, who lives within every Christian (Romans 8:9), is God's mark of ownership in our lives, showing that we belong to Jesus. Paul also refers to the Holy Spirit as a down payment or deposit that guarantees that the rest of the money will definitely be paid in the future. His activity in our lives is a foretaste of heaven, guaranteeing that one day we will receive our final inheritance.

God uses two other factors to bring us an assurance that we belong to Jesus.

➢ The first has to do with what Jesus achieved on the cross. On the basis of Jesus' death, God has forgiven all our sins, freed us from sin's control and has had His anger against us pacified. The Bible states that, if we place our trust in Jesus, we will experience forgiveness, freedom and friendship with God. Jesus' resurrection is God's stamp of approval on Jesus' death and His confirmation that it did achieve what the Bible said it would achieve. Our assurance does not depend on anything we have done or will ever do, but it depends entirely on Jesus and what He did on the Cross.

➤ The other strand is the Father's word. Granted that our assurance depends on Jesus' death, how can we know that, when we placed our trust in Jesus, we were forgiven, set free and became God's friends? God says so. He has promised to give salvation to anyone who believes in Jesus (John 3:16, John 3:36, John 6:47, Acts 10:43, Acts 13:39 and 1 John 5:12). Assurance of salvation is a question of having faith in what God has said, even against all the evidence of our senses. We may not feel that we are Christians, but trusting in the bare Word of a promise-making and promise-keeping God will ultimately bring us assurance. Just as the objective reality of the cross justifies us in God's sight, so the objective reality of God's promises of salvation brings us an assurance of salvation. The blood makes us safe and the written Word makes us sure (1 John 5:13).

❖ **BY TEACHING US ABOUT JESUS**

Although He clearly believed that His teaching was of monumental significance and that His actions were momentously important, Jesus never wrote down anything of what He said and did. The reason why He never committed His teaching to paper or wrote an autobiography is that He anticipated the teaching activity of the Holy Spirit. On the night before His death, Jesus promised His disciples that the Holy Spirit would help them write down what He had said and done and the implications of His teaching and actions (John 14:26 and John 16:12-15).

Jesus' promise was fulfilled in the writing of the New Testament. The Holy Spirit's reminding ministry led to the Four Gospels as He helped Matthew, Mark, Luke and John recall Jesus' words and actions. The Holy Spirit's teaching ministry led to the New Testament letters as He enabled the New Testament writers to come to a full understanding of Jesus' person and work.

> Jesus' promise in John 14:26 and 16:12-15 has been twisted to mean that people today can set the Bible to one side because the Holy Spirit will lead people today into new truths. However, this interpretation of Jesus' promise has lost the plot somewhere down the line. For a start, Jesus' promise was primarily directed towards the apostles. The "you" of John 14:26 and 16:13 refers to them. It is true that about 90% of what Jesus said that night before His execution applies to every Christian, but not all of it does. The primary focus of the other 10% was the apostles. This promise is one that falls into the 10% category. Also Jesus promised that the Holy Spirit would guide the apostles into *all* truth, not just some truth that needed to be supplemented by future new truths.

The Holy Spirit still has a teaching ministry directed towards Christians today. However, the emphasis has changed. He taught the apostles, and the apostles alone, new truths. What He does with us is to lead us into a deeper understanding of the truth He taught the apostles. He does not teach us anything that He did not teach the apostles. His ministry to them was one of *revelation*, making the truth known to them, and *inspiration*, helping them to write down revealed truth in words that were free from any errors. His teaching ministry towards us is one of *illumination*, giving us a clearer grasp of the meaning and implications of the truth already revealed and written down in the Bible.

The Holy Spirit also has a reminding ministry directed towards Christians today. He reminds us of the Bible's directions and promises. For example, we have a choice to make, and we are not sure what path to take. Then we remember a Bible verse, or a biblical principle, or the story of someone from the Bible who faced a similar dilemma, and we know what direction to go.

> The Holy Spirit was not given to pander to our laziness. He will not remind us of biblical directions, promises and principles we have never read or learnt. This is where regular and systematic Bible reading kicks in. It enables us to build up a store of data from which the Holy Spirit can retrieve the Bible directions and promises He wants to use in His reminding ministry.

❖ **BY CREATING AND NURTURING IN US A LOVE FOR JESUS**

The Holy Spirit's regenerating activity not only transforms our opinion of Jesus (2 Corinthians 5:16), it also revolutionises the way we feel about Jesus. Once we hated Him, but now we love Jesus. Our new feelings of love for Jesus are something that the Holy Spirit creates in us (Romans 5:5). However, He wants us to love Jesus more and more, so He nurtures our love for Jesus. As we read the Bible, pray, worship with other Christians and participate in the Lord's Supper, the Holy Spirit helps us see the breathtaking attractiveness of His character and the astounding graciousness of what He did for us, and so deepens our love for Jesus.

We express this Spirit-created and Spirit-nurtured love for Jesus, first and foremost, by obeying Him (John 14:15). This is the acid test of our love for Jesus – do we put into practice the Bible's teaching? However, love touches our emotions as well as driving our wills, so we also exhibit our love for Jesus by praising Him. Like a husband who is always going on about his wife, so we will want to constantly applaud our Saviour's character and achievements (Psalm 63:2-5, Psalm 103:1-13 and Psalm 145:1-8).

It is essential that both praise and obedience are in tandem in our lives. Obedience without praise turns the Christian life into a grim slog and a soul-destroying grind, while praise without obedience is just hot air and empty words.

❖ BY MAKING US MORE LIKE JESUS

In His relentless pursuit to glorify Jesus, the Holy Spirit not only brings us to experience Jesus' life within us, He also sets about reproducing Jesus' character in us. This is God's overarching plan for our lives (Romans 8:29). By showing us in the Bible how God wants us to live (Psalm 119:105), by helping us to overcome all the external and internal barriers we face as we try to do what God wants (1 John 4:4), and by teaching us to pray so that, through prayer, we access God's power to enable us to actually do what the Bible teaches (Romans 8:26), the Holy Spirit produces "the Fruit of the Spirit" (Galatians 5:22-23) in us. "The Fruit of the Spirit" is nothing less than Jesus' character, because no one ever exhibited these qualities in such balance and to such perfection as Jesus did.

Various attempts have been made to classify the nine flavours that Paul blends together to make up "the Fruit of the Spirit". Perhaps the simplest is to take them as three sets of three. The qualities of love, joy and peace have to do with our relationship with God. Love leads the way because it is the greatest of all Christian qualities (1 Corinthians 13:13). We have been on the receiving end of God's undeserved and sacrificial love (Romans 5:8 and Ephesians 5:2 and 25). We will try to love others in the way God has loved us. On the surface, joy appears to be the Christian parallel to humanistic happiness, but they are only very distantly related. Happiness depends on circumstances. If things are going well, people love it, but when things go badly, they become down. Joy is based on something unchanging – who God is and what Jesus has done. This is why we can experience God's joy in our hearts even when we are going through great trials. Peace is a sense of calmness. We experience peace, not because we ignore the reality of our situation, but because we know that God is in control and we commit the situation to Him in prayer (Philippians 4:6-7).

The qualities of patience, kindness and goodness point to our relationship with others. Patience puts up with all sorts of aggravation from others. Kindness is not simply a refusal to retaliate; it is a desire to actually do good towards those who are giving us grief. It is goodness that turns desire into action. It is a sleeves-rolled-up quality that tries to serve others in a concrete, constructive way.

The qualities of faithfulness, gentleness and self-control highlight our relationship with ourselves. Faithfulness is a solid, dependable trustworthiness. We can be relied on to keep our promises and not to leave tasks unfinished. Gentleness is not another term for softness or weakness. It is the opposite of self-seeking. We do not do things for what we can get out of it and the buzz it gives us. Instead we do what we do in order to help and serve others. Self-control is being able to manage our minds, tongues and behaviour.

Notice that Paul uses a singular term – "fruit" – to describe these nine qualities. This implies that we cannot pick and choose which of these qualities we want to display. We are to exhibit all nine of them. When we do that, we become more and more like Jesus.

How can these qualities be developed? We cannot produce them ourselves. In fact, we naturally produce the opposite (Galatians 5:19-21). These qualities are the harvest that the Holy Spirit cultivates in our lives, and that is why they are "the Fruit of the *Spirit*". If they are to be seen in us, then we need to go along with the Spirit's leading in our lives (Galatians 5:25). They are "the *Fruit* of the Spirit", so like any other type of fruit, they will only develop given the right conditions. We must not think that just because the reproduction of Jesus' character in our lives is the product of the Holy Spirit's activity that there is nothing for us to

122

do. We are to sow to the Spirit (Galatians 6:7-8). Sowing to the Spirit is a reference to our lifestyle. It includes the books we read, the company we keep, the friendships we cultivate, the movies we watch, the pursuits that occupy our leisure time, and everything that absorbs our energy and dominates our minds. If we go after what is good (Philippians 4:8), our lives will provide fertile soil in which the Holy Spirit can grow these nine delightful qualities.

❖ **BY HELPING US TO LIVE FOR JESUS**

Becoming a Christian is initially exciting, however, it does not take us long to realise that living for Jesus is far from easy. In fact, the further we travel down the road of following Jesus, the harder it becomes. How can we live for Jesus in an increasingly hostile environment? We can't unless the Holy Spirit helps us.

On the night before His death, as He met with His disciples for a few moments of peace and quiet before the maelstrom of His arrest, trial and execution, Jesus' great concern was that His followers would be able to live for Him once He was no longer physically present with them. So He promised the Holy Spirit's help (John 14:16). He described the Holy Spirit as "another Counsellor". This word "counsellor" began life as a legal word. If you were hauled up before the courts, it was used of the lawyer who defended you, or a witness who spoke up on your behalf, or a friend who came along to give you moral support. With time, the word developed a wider usage. It came to mean someone who helped in any way. As the Counsellor, the Holy Spirit is going to give us all the assistance we need to live for Jesus in the nuts and bolts of our everyday situation.

When the Mad Hatter offered Alice another cup of tea, she was annoyed and pointed out that she could not have another cup of tea because she had not had one in the first place. So, when Jesus says that the Holy Spirit is going to act as "**another** Counsellor" to His disciples (John 14:16), He was implying that they had already benefited from the help of a previous

Counsellor, and that Counsellor, of which the Holy Spirit was to be another Counsellor, was Jesus Himself. Although distinct from Jesus, the Holy Spirit is another Jesus to Christians. He is to us today everything that Jesus was to His disciples while He was on earth. He helped them when they were troubled, strengthened them when they were tempted, comforted them when they were worried, filled them with joy when they were sad, gave them guidance when they were uncertain what to do, and straightened out their thinking when they were puzzled and confused. As Jesus' other self, the Holy Spirit is to us what Jesus was to them.

Some Christians wish they could climb into a time machine and go back to the time when Jesus was on earth. "It must have been great to have been with Jesus as He did all those miracles and said all those wonderful things," they say with misty-eyes. This kind of nostalgia is natural but mistaken. We are at an advantage over those who only knew Jesus in the flesh (John 16:7), because we have the Holy Spirit. For a start, Jesus can now be with every Christian. While physically present on earth, He could only be with a limited amount of people at any one given point in time, but now, through the Holy Spirit, Jesus can be present with every Christian all of the time. It is of more help to us to have the Holy Spirit than to have Jesus' physical presence because, through the Holy Spirit, Jesus is now present continually and universally.

❖ **BY ENABLING US TO SERVE JESUS**

In his speech when he was inaugurated as President of the United States of America, John F Kennedy challenged the American people not to ask what their country could do for them, but what they could do for their country. In the years since JFK spoke those words, society has become more and more self-centred. For people today, who are obsessed with looking after Number One, serving others is not on their agenda. Christians are called to buck the trend and instead of just watching out for themselves, to serve others. In order to enable us to serve, Jesus has given every Christian at least one gift or ability (Ephesians 4:7 and 1 Peter 4:10). Sometimes the adjective "spiritual" is used to describe these gifts and abilities (1 Corinthians 12:1). That label is not meant to suggest that Jesus gives Christians certain gifts while the Holy Spirit gives us a separate set of gifts. Nor is it meant to imply that there is a clear-cut differentiation between the abilities we brought with us into our Christian lives and the abilities we develop after we became Christians. The attachment "spiritual" is used to indicate that it is only as the Holy Spirit energises us in the use of our gifts and abilities that Jesus will be glorified.

Amid the many controversies that rage in the church about spiritual gifts (How many are there? Have some ceased?), several points of agreement stand out. No Christian is giftless (1 Corinthians 12:7 and Ephesians 4:7). It is the responsibility of each Christian to find out, develop and fully use whatever capacities for service God has given him or her. It is also the job of the church's leadership to facilitate service opportunities for every Christian so that the gifts Jesus has given the church can be utilised (Ephesians 4:11-12). It is also clear that, while some Christians are multi-talented, having been given many gifts, no one Christian has a monopoly of all the gifts (1 Corinthians 12:8-10). This is why, when spiritual gifts are mentioned, the body metaphor is used to describe the church (Romans 12:4-8, 1 Corinthians 12:14-30 and Ephesians 4:12). Serving Jesus is a team effort, with each Christian pulling together in the use of the abilities God has given.

The New Testament indicates that a spiritual gift is not for the individual Christian's personal enjoyment. Jesus gave them so that His church would be built up (Ephesians 4:11-13). From the Romans 12:6-8 catalogue, the church is strengthened and matured as gifts related to speech and gifts related to loving, practical helpfulness are utilised. When he lists these spiritual gifts, Paul alternates between the two categories, and the alternating pattern is designed to put to bed the idea that some gifts are better than others. However much gifts may differ, all are of equal dignity as they all build up the church. The only question is whether we properly use the gift we have (1 Peter 4:10-11).

How can you discover what spiritual gift you might have?

➢ Explore the possibilities. Study the list of gifts in the New Testament. Know what options are open to you. Pray that you will be open to the Holy Spirit's guidance through the Word.

➢ Exercise what you think your gift might be. You might think God has given you a certain gift. You will only discover if that is the case by carrying out the tasks associated with it. For example, if you think you have the gift of explaining the Bible in a way that helps people see how it relates to everyday life, ask if you could help with leading a Bible study group.

➢ Examine your feelings. If you find yourself disliking the task involved in exercising a gift, that might be an indication that God has not given it to you.

➢ Evaluate your effectiveness. Each spiritual gift is designed to accomplish some specific objective. If you get no appropriate results from doing the task associated with a gift, you may not have that gift.

➢ Expect confirmation from others. Gifts are not discovered or developed in isolation. If you have a gift, other Christians will recognise that fact. Ask the opinion of others, especially the elders in your church. If you think you have a gift, but no one else agrees with you, be very suspicious of your conclusions about your gifts.

❖ BY EMPOWERING US IN OUR WITNESS TO JESUS

Jesus' last words to His disciples before He went back into heaven, as recorded by Matthew and Luke, show His concern that they should witness to others about Him (Matthew 28:19 and Acts 1:8). This was a daunting task because society was not at all sympathetic to Jesus' claims to be God's Son and the only Saviour. However, coupled with this challenge to take the good news of the Christian message to all parts of the world was Jesus' promise of the Holy Spirit's power for the task (Matthew 28:20 and Acts 1:8).

The fact that Jesus gave the gift of the Holy Spirit to empower us in our witness to Him is underlined in John 15:26-27. One of the Spirit's tasks would be to bear witness to Jesus. In a sense, His is the only witness to Jesus that ultimately matters. Only the Holy Spirit can open spiritually blind eyes so that they see the truth about Jesus. Only the Holy Spirit can give life to the spiritually dead so that they can believe in Jesus. Only the Holy Spirit can change the spiritual direction of people's lives so that, instead of going their own way, they begin to follow Jesus and submit to His control. The Holy Spirit witnesses to Jesus through our witness. In one breath, Jesus speaks about the Holy Spirit's witnessing activity (John 15:26) and then, in the next breath, He speaks about our witnessing activity (John 15:27).

If you have ever thought your witness to Jesus was a bit feeble, then join the club. Most of us feel we do not properly answer the questions people ask us. Afterwards we think of a good answer and say to ourselves, "If only I had thought of that at the time!" However, Jesus has promised us the Spirit's power. So no matter how feeble or inadequate we might consider our witness to Jesus to be, the Holy Spirit will speak through us, and it is His testimony that really counts.

What then are the signs that Jesus' unpretentious Spirit is at work? It is not the existence of mystical and ecstatic experience, nor visions and supposed direct revelations from God, nor even healings, tongues and apparent miracles. Satan, playing on our fallenness, can counterfeit all these things (Colossians 2:18 and 2 Thessalonians 2:9-12). When the Spirit is active, Jesus will be glorified.

- People will come to know Jesus as their Saviour and Lord.
- People will be humbly certain that they are Christians.
- People will be growing in their understanding of the Bible's teaching and its relevancy for contemporary living.
- People will love Jesus more and more, and seek to express that love in obedience and praise.
- People will increasingly become like Jesus in their thinking, speech and behaviour.
- People will be helped to live for Jesus in their homes and places of study, work and recreation.
- People will be enabled to serve Jesus and empowered to witness to Him.

These are the biblical indicators by which we can judge whether the Holy Spirit is at work in an individual or a church.

DIGGING DEEPER

You might like to explore further some of the issues raised in this chapter by reading *The Holy Spirit* by Sinclair Ferguson (Published by IVP), *Keep in Step with the Spirit* by J.I. Packer (Published by IVP) and *The Mystery of the Holy Spirit* by R.C. Sproul (Published by Christian Focus Publications).

10. THE BIG IDEA

In this chapter, we are going to discover what the Bible says about the Covenant of Grace.
GOD THE FATHER IS THE PRIME MOVER OF THE COVENANT OF GRACE
SALVATION IS THE PROMISE OF THE COVENANT OF GRACE
JESUS IS THE MEDIATOR OF THE COVENANT OF GRACE
THE HOLY SPIRIT IS THE EXECUTOR OF THE COVENANT OF GRACE
FAITH IN AND OBEDIENCE TO JESUS ARE THE OBLIGATIONS OF THE COVENANT OF GRACE

A youth leader once set a group of fourteen year olds the task of doing a jigsaw. They were unable to complete the puzzle, not because some of the pieces were missing, but because she refused to show them the finished picture. For some Christians the Bible can be like a jigsaw with no picture. They know that all the bits are there, but they cannot work out how everything hangs together. We have looked at several individual components of the Bible's teaching; we now need to see how they fit together. The unifying theme that connects all its separate parts is known as "the Covenant of Grace."

Although the word "covenant" is not part of our everyday vocabulary, we are familiar with the ideas that lie behind it. A hire purchase agreement, a learning contract, an exchange of marriage vows, a will, a peace treaty, an arrangement that ends a political or industrial dispute and a business deal are all contemporary examples of a covenant. "Covenant" pulls words such as "agreement," "promise," "commitment," "obligation" and "arrangement" into its orbit. If we apply these concepts to the Covenant of Grace, it points to the fact that it is an agreement God makes with us, in which He commits Himself to bless us, and, in return, He places us under obligation to trust in His promises and to obey His commands.

At first glance, it might appear that God makes many

covenants with various individuals and groups of people such as His covenant with Noah, with Abraham, with the nation of Israel at Mount Sinai, with David and the New Covenant. However, these are not different, separate and unrelated covenants but developing aspects of a single Covenant of Grace. God is progressively unfolding His covenant until it reaches a climax in the New Covenant.

I know that statistics can be used to prove almost anything, but let me give some to back up my claim that the Covenant of Grace is the Bible's big idea.

➢ The word "covenant" appears 271 times in the Bible, all the way from Genesis 6:18 to Revelation 11:19.

➢ The Lord (usually set in small capitals in most Bible versions), God's special covenant name, is the most common description of Him in the Old Testament, occurring 5655 times.

➢ The catchphrase of the Covenant of Grace is "I will be their God" or "I will be your God." It is scattered throughout all the different parts of the Bible, first in Genesis 17:8 and finally in Revelation 21:3.

➢ The terms "your God" and "our God" have heavy covenantal overtones, and they are found 685 times in the Bible, beginning at Genesis 17:7 and ending with Revelation 19:5.

I do not want to overwhelm you with stats, but you can see that this theme of the Covenant of Grace turns up throughout the Bible. The claim that it is the Bible's big idea has a great deal going for it.

---

1. GOD THE FATHER IS THE PRIME MOVER OF THE COVENANT OF GRACE

This is something the Bible constantly underlines. We did not come looking for God; He took the initiative and came looking for us. The first move always lies with God. The capacity we have to enjoy a personal relationship with God is itself a gift from Him (Ecclesiastes 3:11). We only know what God is like, how we can be in a right relationship with Him, and how to live in a way that pleases Him because God took the initiative to tell us (John 1:18 and 2 Timothy 3:15-17). Our failure to love God and our rebellion against God created a massive obstacle between Him and us (Isaiah 59:2). We do not have what it takes to get over this obstruction, but God did what we could not do. He sent Jesus to die in order to bulldoze the roadblock (Colossians 1:21-22). We only experience God's salvation because God has gone after us and wooed us to Himself (John 6:44 and 1 John 4:19). The only reason why we will arrive safely in heaven is because God never leaves anything He starts unfinished (Philippians 1:6).

God's continual initiative is the reason why the adjective "grace" is attached to God's covenant. He did not have to do all these things in our lives. There was nothing attractive about us that forced God to come after us. In fact, the exact opposite was true. Everything about us was screaming out for God's judgment, but instead He loved us, giving us the pardon and forgiveness we did not deserve and withholding from us the punishment we did deserve.

In *The Lion, the Witch and the Wardrobe*, when the children discover that Aslan, the King of Narnia, is a lion, Susan asks if Aslan is safe. "Safe?" said Mr Beaver. "Who said anything about safe? Of course, he isn't safe. But he's good." In C.S. Lewis' stories about Narnia, Aslan represents Jesus. Lewis is saying that following Jesus is not cosy, but often unnerving and uncomfortable. God continues to take the initiative in our lives even when we have become Christians, nudging us out of our Christian comfort zone into arenas of service and witness where our faith will be stretched, and our experience of His strength deepened.

2. SALVATION IS THE PROMISE OF THE COVENANT OF GRACE

We can see this in the covenant promises God made to Abraham (Genesis 17:1-14). From a surface scan it would seem that God promised Abraham children and land. However, that would be a misreading of God's promises. Although they had physical aspects to them, they were primarily spiritual, and this is indicated by the way they are tied up in the phrase "I will be your God" (Genesis 17:7). This phrase is like an icon on my computer, when clicked, it acts as a gateway that allows me to access other programs. When we click on the phrase "I will be your God", we discover that it opens up God's promise to bring us into a right relationship with Him (Genesis 15:6 and Romans 4:1-6), to make us His friends (James 2:23), to put His Holy Spirit within us so that we have the willingness and ability to obey His Word (Jeremiah 31:33-34 and Ezekiel 36:25-27), to be with us always (Matthew 28:20), and to take us to heaven to be with Him forever when we die (Revelation 21:1-4). God's promises are breathtaking in their scope, securing forgiveness for the past, assuring us of power for the present, and filling us with hope for the future.

The people to whom God made these promises of salvation also highlight how gracious He is. Throughout the Old Testament, our attention is drawn to the fact that God made these promises to sinful, weak human beings. For example, in Genesis 9:1-19, we read of God entering into a covenant with Noah, and then immediately afterwards, in Genesis 9:20-23, we come across the sorry story of how Noah got drunk. In Genesis 12:1-3, we find God making staggering promises to Abraham, and then, in Genesis 12:12-20, we read of the shabby way in which Abraham puts Sarah's life in danger in order to save his own skin by pretending she was his sister, and not his wife. These people did not earn the right to be on the receiving end of God's promises of salvation, yet God graciously entered into covenant with them.

However, there is more, because in the Old Testament we not only unearth the fact that God entered into covenant with sinners, He also entered into covenant with their descendants. God's promises were made to Noah and his descendants (Genesis 9:9), and to Abraham and his descendants (Genesis 17:7 and 10). In Old Testament times, the old administration of the Covenant of Grace, the principle of God's promise being "to you and your descendants" clearly operated, and it still does today in New Testament times, the new administration of the Covenant of Grace, In his sermon on the Day of Pentecost, Peter uses Joel 2:28-32 as a launch pad to spell out the differences between the old and new administrations of the covenant. Then, in the context of highlighting the changes, Peter announces that one covenantal pattern continues over from the old to the new, and it is that God's promises are "for you and your children, and for all who are far off – for all whom the Lord our God will call" (Acts 2:39). Many old covenantal patterns have been brushed aside with the arrival of the new covenant, but one has not – God's promise is to the believer and his children.

For those of us who live in a western culture, with its emphasis on the individual, it might be hard for us to get our heads around the idea that, on the basis of his faith, the believer's children are also the focus of God's promises. However, this idea is not as foreign to our way of thinking as it might appear at first glance. I am a British citizen, not because I was born in the United Kingdom for I was born in Nigeria, but because my father is a British citizen. My British citizenship was determined by his British citizenship. So believers' children are drawn into the orbit of God's covenantal promises because of their parents' faith in Jesus. Christians' children are not outsiders, but insiders, part of the covenant community.

3. JESUS IS THE MEDIATOR OF THE COVENANT OF GRACE

For us, making a promise is quite a different matter to delivering that promise, whereas for God, it is no problem (Daniel 4:35). The delivery of His covenant promises centres on Jesus, and especially His death. Jesus Himself saw His death from

134

that angle (Matthew 26:27-28). In my will, I have promised that Martyn, my son, will inherit a grandfather clock that has been in the Crooks family for several generations. However, it will not become his until I die. In the same way, Jesus had to die for God's covenant promises of salvation to be realised (Hebrews 9:16). God's promise of forgiveness rested on Jesus' death (Hebrews 9:22). His promise of the Holy Spirit also depended on Jesus dying (John 7:37-39 – in John's Gospel Jesus being glorified is almost a technical term for Jesus' death). Our hope of heaven is based upon what Jesus achieved on the cross (Hebrews 10:19-20).

In the Bible, Jesus is depicted as the last Adam, who would succeed where the first Adam failed, and by His perfect obedience secure eternal life for His people (Romans 5:19). All the Old Testament sacrifices, religious festivals, rituals and institutions such as the priesthood, the position of king and the role of prophet pointed to Jesus and His death. The Old Testament anticipated Jesus, and the New Testament states that Jesus the Mediator has come.

4. THE HOLY SPIRIT IS THE EXECUTOR OF THE COVENANT OF GRACE

Several of my friends are in the legal profession, and they are often asked to act as executor for clients who make a will. It means that, when their clients die, they are responsible for ensuring that the money and property are divided out in the way stipulated under the terms of the will. If God the Father masterminded the Covenant of Grace and Jesus secured the covenant promises by His death, then it is the role of the Holy Spirit to make the covenant blessings take root in the lives of those with whom God has entered into covenant.

In the work of salvation, the Father, Son and Holy Spirit work together. This has lead theologians to suggest that lying behind the Covenant of Grace is what they call "The Covenant of Redemption." It was the before-time foundation for the historical Covenant of Grace. From eternity past, God as Father, Son and Holy Spirit had a strategy as to how He would save sinful people. The Father planned salvation, and that would involve the Son becoming a real human being (Hebrews 2:14), perfectly keeping God's Law (Galatians 4:4) and dying as a substitute for sinners (Isaiah 53:5-6). The Son would carry out His Father's plan by coming to earth to die, and in order to carry out His mission, the Father would prepare a body for Him (Hebrews 10:5), empower Him with the Spirit so He could do His work (Isaiah 42:1 and John 3:34) and rescue Him from death (Psalm 16:8-11). The Holy Spirit would then make the Son's achievements real in people's experience.

It is not hard to see how the Holy Spirit is the Executor of the Covenant of Grace, making its promised blessings real in our experience. Take the covenant promise of being right with God. It is the Holy Spirit who generates the faith that Christians need in order to trust in Jesus and be saved (Ephesians 2:8). He gave Old Testament believers the faith to look *forward* to Jesus, and He gives New Testament Christians the faith to look *back* to Jesus. Another covenant promise is power to live as God's children, and it is the Holy Spirit who reassures us that we are part of God's Family (Romans 8:14-16) and who helps us to behave as God's children should (Galatians 5:16). The future covenant promise is the hope of heaven, and it is the Holy Spirit who guarantees that when we die we will go to be with Jesus (Romans 8:23-24 and Ephesians 4:30).

5. FAITH IN AND OBEDIENCE TO JESUS ARE THE OBLIGATIONS OF THE COVENANT OF GRACE

God's initiative should never minimise the importance of our response. We have certain covenant obligations.

We are to believe the covenant promises. We are to follow Abraham's example, who believed what God promised him. In faith, he looked forward to Jesus and what He would achieve when He came to die. As a result of trusting in Jesus, Abraham began to enjoy the covenant blessings (Genesis 15:6). We are also to obey the covenant regulations. God expects us to live in a certain way. We are to do what He says in His Word so that His reputation is enhanced. This obedience is not an optional extra for those who are keen. It is something every Christian is to do.

The practical teaching of the Bible as to how we should live is always set within a covenantal framework.

➤ Take, for example, the Ten Commandments. God begins with a statement that is just saturated in covenantal terminology (Exodus 20:2), and then goes on to tell us how we should behave towards Him (Exodus 20:3-11) and others (Exodus 20:12-17). Our obedience to the Ten Commandments is not a pathetic attempt to earn God's salvation. It is our response of love to His saving initiative.

➤ Take also the covenantal structure of passages such as Ephesians 4-6 and Colossians 3-4, in which Paul spells out how Christians should live. He does not dive straight in and tell us what we should do. Instead he spends time writing about what God has done for us in Jesus (Ephesians 1-3 and Colossians 1-2). Only after he has done that does Paul explain how we should live. Once more the idea that our obedience is our response of love to God's saving initiative is underscored.

The idea of the Covenant of Grace is the Bible's big idea. It is the picture that helps us see how all the individual pieces of the Bible fit together. Once we get our heads round the idea of the Covenant of Grace, it will jump out at us from every part of the Bible. The theme will be so ever-present that we will scratch our heads and wonder why we never saw it before.

However, the Covenant of Grace is not only the key to

understanding God's Word, it also brings consistency into our relationship with God. We know where we stand with Him, because He always acts within the framework of the Covenant of Grace. He does not behave irrationally or unpredictably. His ways with us do not change. We know that if we honour Him by obeying the Bible and loving His Son with all our being, He will bless us. We also know that if we do not honour Him, then a completely opposite scenario comes into play. We do not have to guess where we stand with God; He has told us in His Word.

This theme should also fill us with amazement at God's momentous grace. God, who is the almighty Creator and sovereign King of the universe, has committed Himself to loving and blessing *us*! He has opened up His heart to us (Genesis 18:17), called us His friends (John 15:13-15), and made us colleagues in His work (2 Corinthians 6:1). What is even more staggering is that God's deliberate decision to commit Himself to love and bless us is based on His perfect knowledge of us. He knows the worst about us, yet this has not disillusioned Him about us or put Him off in His determination to save us, change us and bring us to be with Him forever.

DIGGING DEEPER

You might like to explore further some of the issues raised in this chapter by reading *Covenants: God's way with His people* by O Palmer Robertson (Published by Great Commission Publications) and *Learning from the Old Testament* by Allan Harman (Published by Christian Focus Publications).

11. WHO NEEDS IT?

In this chapter, we are going to discover what the Bible says about the church.
WHAT THE CHURCH IS
- **The church is engaged in spiritual warfare while on earth and destined for ultimate victory in heaven**
  - **The church is visible and invisible**
  - **The church is worldwide and local**
  - **The church is an organisation and an organism**
WHAT THE CHURCH DOES
- **The church reaches up to God in worship**
Worship is to be God-centred, Jesus-exalting, Spirit-empowered, Bible-regulated, personality-engaging, culturally-relevant, love-driven and life-impacting
- **The church reaches out to others in mission**
The what, where, who and why of mission
  - **The church reaches in to each other in fellowship**

Surveys point out that, while people find Jesus attractive and fascinating, they are deeply suspicious of organised religion. As Jamie, a sixteen-year-old from a totally unchurched background, said to one of my friends, "Jesus rocks but His mates stink". It is the church, with all its scandals and in-fighting, that bothers people, so they don't bother with it.

I want to defend the church, not because I have a vested interest in the church as it provides me with work and its members pay my salary, but because God is on the side of the church. God paid a high price for the church (Acts 20:28). No father ever loved his son as God the Father loved Jesus, yet He gave His Son up to death, even to the point of abandoning Him (Matthew 27:46), in order that the church might be rescued from sin's penalty and control. Jesus' mission to earth had a specific goal – to die for the sins of the church, His people (Matthew 1:21 and Ephesians 5:25).

The creation of the church was at the heart of God's plan of salvation. The church was no afterthought on God's part. It was not God's Plan B. God's strategy, which He formulated before time began, was not to save lots of isolated, unconnected individuals, but to form His redeemed people into one unit – the church. The Bible's metaphors for the church as being the body, the army, the family and the building call attention to this. They carry with them this idea of individuals formed into a unit.

The church is the soil in which our faith in Jesus grows. Luke records how, as a result of Peter's Spirit-empowered preaching on the Day of Pentecost, 3000 people became Christians (Acts 2:41). Then he immediately goes on to describe how these people progressed in their new faith (Acts 2:42). It took place within the setting of the church. It was no accident that the Holy Spirit guided Luke to place these two verses side-by-side as He wanted to flag up the principle that He uses what goes on within the church to develop our faith. For example, the Holy Spirit wants to cultivate qualities such as love and patience in us. However, these virtues cannot develop in isolation as we cannot become more loving unless there are other people to serve, and we cannot learn patience unless we come into contact with other people who have the potential to irritate us. When you come across people who are balanced and mature Christians, you can be almost 100% certain that they are up to their elbows in their church's life and work.

If all this is true, then to dump the church would be crazy. We would be devaluing something God counts as valuable, marginalizing something God considers as central, and neglecting something God tells us is vital for our spiritual well-being. To refuse to go with the flow and start to bother with the church might be one of the smartest moves we ever made because it would help our Christian development enormously and put us right at the heart of what God is doing in the world.

1. WHAT THE CHURCH IS

If you think that finishing off the sentence "The church is …" is child's play, then take a look at these three statements. "If you take the first left and then immediately go right, you will come to the church". "I am a member of the Presbyterian Church in Ireland". "What time is church at tonight?" Did you notice how each of them used the word "church" in a different way? In the first statement, it means a building located in a specific setting; in the second, a denomination, and in the third, a meeting when people gather together. Getting a handle on the church is a little more complex than first meets the eye.

Primarily the church must be seen in terms of relationships, and not buildings or organisational structures. The church is made up of people who are, first and foremost, related to God. They are the people whom God the Father, by the Holy Spirit's activity, has invited to belong to Jesus (1 Peter 2:4-5 and 9-10). Then, as a consequence of this common relationship with God, the church consists of people who are related to each other.

When was the church's birthday? "That's easy," people reply "The Day of Pentecost". However, if the church is comprised of people who are in a relationship with God, then it was in existence long before the Day of Pentecost. There has been a church ever since people trusted in Jesus and so came to know God personally. The first people to do so were Adam and Eve. They believed God's promise of a future Saviour who would come to undo all the tragic consequences of their rebellion against God (Genesis 3:15). The church existed in Old Testament times, because there were people who belonged to Jesus as the Holy Spirit brought them to trust in Jesus – men like Abraham (Genesis 15:6), Job (Job 19:25-27) and David (Psalm 32:1-5), and women like Ruth (Ruth 1:16). Recently Rosie, my oldest daughter, turned eighteen. As far as UK law is concerned, she is now an adult, and can enjoy all sorts of wonderful privileges she did not

142

> have as a minor – the right to vote, take out a bank loan and serve on a jury! To use an old fashioned phrase, she has come of age. The Day of Pentecost was not the church's birthday, but its coming of age. As a result of the Spirit's coming, the post-Pentecost church enjoys greater blessings than the pre-Pentecost church - a fuller revelation of God and His ways (Hebrews 1:1-2 and John 16:13), a greater freedom (Galatians 4:1-7 and 2 Corinthians 3:17), and a wider membership of both Jews and non-Jews (Isaiah 2:2-3 and Acts 15:12-17).

❖ THE CHURCH IS ENGAGED IN SPIRITUAL WARFARE WHILE ON EARTH AND DESTINED FOR ULTIMATE VICTORY IN HEAVEN

While we are alive, Christians are engaged in persistent combat with three enemies who are traditionally referred to as the world, the flesh and the devil. By "the world" the Bible means secular society that leaves God out of the picture. It is not neutral, but constantly trying to squeeze us into its mould (Romans 12:2) as it daily puts pressure on us to adopt a self-centred perspective on life and a pleasure-orientated lifestyle (2 Timothy 3:2-4). By "the flesh" the Bible means our sinful nature that remains within us even after we have become Christians, engaging in an unrelenting guerrilla war against us. It does its worst to stop us doing what is right and seduces us into doing what is wrong (Romans 7:19). Its attacks are continuous, fierce and devastating. Behind the world and the flesh, pulling the strings, is the dark, sinister, evil figure of Satan, the devil. "The Church Militant" is the time-honoured term used to describe the church on earth as it engages in spiritual warfare against the world, the flesh and the devil.

One day, when we die and go to be with Jesus, our spiritual warfare will come to an end. In heaven there is no world, no flesh or no devil, so we will be able to rest from all our spiritual combat (Revelation 14:13). The term "The Church Triumphant" is used to describe the church in heaven, which has overcome its spiritual opponents.

> When they have to struggle against the world, the flesh and the devil, some Christians, especially new ones, think that there is something wrong with their Christian lives. They imagine that no one else faces the pressure and experiences the temptations that they do. However, engaging in spiritual warfare is normal Christian experience. It comes with the territory, and all Christians battle each day against the world, the flesh and the devil (1 Corinthians 10:13). To help us in our fight, God has provided us with all the equipment and resources we need so that we can stand firm in our spiritual struggles (Ephesians 6:10-18).

❖ **THE CHURCH IS VISIBLE AND INVISIBLE**

This distinction applies to the church on earth. The visible church is the church as we see it, made up of people who claim to be Christians, along with their children, and, at the present time, their lifestyle appears to back it up. However, Jesus taught that, in the visible church, there would be people who are impostors (Matthew 7:15-27 and Matthew 13:47-50). The visible church / invisible church distinction takes into account this fact, for the invisible church is the church as God sees it. Only He knows who are genuine from among all those who claim to be Christians.

> This distinction between the visible and invisible church challenges us to look at our own lives to see if there is any evidence to back up our claim that we are Christians (2 Corinthians 13:5 and 2 Peter 1:5-11). If you were put on trial for being a Christian, would there be enough evidence to secure a guilty verdict?

❖ THE CHURCH IS WORLDWIDE AND LOCAL

The visible church is found in every part of the world. God's purpose is to save a people from every nation, culture and language-group (Revelation 5:9 and 7:9), and the make-up of the worldwide church reflects His plan. The church's universality not only has a geographical dimension, but also a social one. The visible church is made up of people from different social, economic, educational and political backgrounds. Being a member of the church does not remove these differences between Christians, but it rises above them. The local church is the localised expression of the worldwide church. Often the word "congregation" is used to describe the local church.

I am shortsighted, so, when I take my glasses off, anything further than 10 metres away is reduced to an indistinct blob. Some churches are spiritually shortsighted. What God is doing in and through other sections of the worldwide church does not excite them. You pick this up from listening to them praying. The focus of their prayers is nearly exclusively on local issues. You sense there is little real interest in the global dimension of the church when you look at their giving patterns, with their money mainly going towards local projects, and especially maintaining buildings.

❖ THE CHURCH IS AN ORGANISATION AND AN ORGANISM

The church has a structure. The Bible's metaphors for the church highlight this reality. A body, an army, a family and a building are all organised in a certain way. God has neither left us to guess what the structure of the church should look like, nor to make up a structure of our own. In the Bible, He has showed us how a congregation should be organised.

Jesus is the Head of the church (Ephesians 4:15, Ephesians 5:23 and Colossians 1:18), ruling it by His Word and Spirit. However, He has delegated the day-to-day running of His church to elders. Rule by elders is the distinctive feature of the way

Presbyterians organise their churches.

Three ideas lie at the core of the Presbyterian structure of organising a church around elders.

➢ The parity of elders. Elders may have different functions, with some ruling and others teaching as well as ruling (1 Timothy 5:17), but, as far as governing the congregation's spiritual life is concerned, all are equal.

➢ The plurality of elders. In each congregation there should always be more than one elder (Acts 14:23 and Titus 1:5). This principle makes sure that leadership in a congregation is shared, not falling on the shoulders of one man but is the responsibility of all the elders acting as a team. Elders are to supervise the spiritual life of the congregation (Acts 20:28). Together, through studying the Bible and prayerfully thinking through its contemporary application, they find out where Jesus wants the congregation to go, and then together they lead God's people in that direction.

➢ Congregations should not exist as autonomous units but are connected to each other. Presbyterianism connects congregations together in various ways. Groups of local churches are organised into a presbytery, several presbyteries into a synod, and all the synods into a General Assembly. This leads to a pooling of resources, with the stronger congregations helping the weaker ones, and so to more effectiveness in mission.

Just in case you are wondering what planet I have been living on for the past forty-six years, I admit that these three ideas are really ideals, and sadly not what happens in practice. The church in our time, like the church throughout the centuries, is made up of sinful leaders whose leadership is often not all that Jesus wants it to be.

146

However, this is not a reason for taking the easy option and giving up on the church. Instead, these three ideas should give us a vision of what the church could be like and should stimulate us to pray for those in leadership in our churches.

The problem with discussing the church's organisation is that it might give the impression that the church is something static, as structures have a nasty habit of becoming rigid and inflexible. However, the Bible also underscores the fact that the church is an organism, something living and dynamic. The body is maturing, the army is on the move, the family is growing, and the building is being constructed. As an organism, the church should be expanding numerically as people become Christians and join it (Acts 2:41, Acts 2:47 and Acts 5:14), and growing spiritually as the inner life of each church member deepens (Ephesians 3:16-19, Philippians 1:9-11 and 2 Thessalonians 1:3).

2. WHAT THE CHURCH DOES

If you asked twenty Christians what they thought the church should be doing, you would probably get twenty different answers. Everyone has an opinion, and is not afraid to state it. When we stop trying to make sure our opinion is heard and take time to listen to Jesus (after all He is the church's King and Head and so His point of view is the only one that ultimately matters), we discover that the Bible instructs the church to be concerned about worship, mission and fellowship.

Some might want to swap around the order of that last sentence and put mission before worship. A case can certainly be made out for doing so, especially the fact that the objective of mission is to produce more worshippers (1 Thessalonians 1:4-10). However, worship is focussed on God, while mission is focussed on human beings, and our responsibilities to God are more important than our responsibilities to other human beings. Also worship is something that will happen in eternity as well as taking

place in time, while mission only goes on in time. Long after
the church's missionary activity is over, its worship will
continue.

❖ THE CHURCH REACHES UP TO GOD IN WORSHIP

Only castaways on a desert island will not be aware that
worship is one of the hot issues within the contemporary church.
It is very touchy subject, for Christians have fallen out with each
other and congregations have split over the issue, disappointing
God and filling Satan with fiendish pleasure. So, when we think
about worship, we need to engage our brains and not allow our
emotions to drive the discussion. What the Bible says about
worship takes us by surprise because it sees worship as something
we do seven days a week, and not just something restricted to
one day a week. According to the Bible, all that we do is worship,
designed to draw attention to how God is loving, great, caring,
powerful, holy and trustworthy (Romans 12:1, 1 Corinthians
10:31 and Colossians 3:23). Although worship is something we
do all the time – what could be called general worship, it is also
something that we do at special times and in particular what we
do when we get together with other Christians on the first day of
the week – what could be called specific worship.

Although I want to concentrate on specific worship, it is
important that we grasp that both these aspects of worship are
closely inter-related. The Old Testament prophets and Jesus
Himself continually stressed that our general worship from
Monday to Saturday dramatically affects our specific worship on
Sunday. On one occasion God says that He hated the worship
His people brought Him because during the rest of the week they
failed to be upfront and honest in their relationships with others,
failed to encourage the exploited, and failed to help the
marginalized (Isaiah 1:11-17). If we want to experience God's life
and power in our specific worship, then we need to make sure
that obedience is the hallmark of our relationship with God, and
that our relationships with others is characterised by generosity,

integrity, humility and honesty.

As we try to tiptoe our way through the minefield that is specific worship, several principles stand out. Worship is to be **God-centred**. The focus of worship is God, and not us (Psalm 29:1-2, Psalm 95:1-2 and 6-7, Psalm 96:1-3 and Psalm 100:1-2 and 3). In worship, we adore God's greatness as we celebrate the magnificent splendour of His character and the stunning graciousness of what He has done in creating, caring for and saving us (Psalm 150:2). God wants us to worship Him (John 4:23), and is constantly inviting us to do so (Matthew 11:28 and James 4:8). We worship to bring pleasure and delight to God (Psalm 147:1,7 and 11), and not for our own benefit. If through our worship we experience blessing, that is a gesture of grace on God's part. We ought not to go to worship God thinking about what we can get out of worship, but asking what we can give to God in worship. If we are going to worship with a "what's-in-this-for-me?" mindset, then we have not started to begin to understand the Bible's teaching about worship.

Worship is to be **Jesus-exalting**. This is the factor that sets apart Christian worship from other types of worship (Philippians 3:3). Christian worship exalts Jesus as it acknowledges that it is only because of what He has done on the cross that we can approach God in worship. Our sins disqualify us from God's presence, but Jesus' death has dealt with them so that we can come close to God (Hebrews 10:19-22). Christian worship also exalts Jesus in that all the elements that go into a service of worship should point to Him. In our singing, we praise Him as our Saviour, Lord and Friend. We pray in His name (John 14:13-14 and John 15:16). Giving our money to God's work is an integral part of our worship, and we do so in response to God's giving of Jesus to us (2 Corinthians 8:9 and 2 Corinthians 9:15). As He is the focal point of the Bible (Luke 24:25-27 and 44-45), no matter what part of God's Word the sermon is based on, it will be about Jesus (1 Corinthians 2:2). If we do not come away from a service of worship with a deeper appreciation of who Jesus is, what He has done for us, and how we can live to please

Him, we have not been involved in Christian worship.

Worship is to be **Spirit-empowered**. Regrettably when many Christians think about worship, words like "dull" and "boring" spring to mind, and most of us have had the unfortunate experience of having sat through at least one mind-numbing, emotion-crushing service. Their solution to this problem is often to advocate abandoning all kinds of structure in a service. The answer, however, is not down that road, but lies in pleading with the Holy Spirit to empower us in our worship, as it is His gracious presence that will stop our services from being sterile and dreary. If we are seeking to exalt Jesus in our worship, then surely the Holy Spirit will give us His power because His supreme delight is to see Jesus glorified.

Worship is to be **Bible-regulated**. When it comes to worship, the Bible issues a spiritual health warning – not all worship pleases God (Isaiah 1:11-17, Amos 5:21-24 and Mark 7:6-7). It is worth pointing out that the Bible says more about worship that is unacceptable to God than it does about worship that brings Him pleasure. The last thing that we want to do is to offend God, so how can we know if our worship fills Him with delight or irritates Him? By going to the Bible, because it is only there that we know what pleases God. The idea that, as long as we are sincere, anything goes in worship is not taught in the Bible, for it warns us that we can be sincerely wrong.

Historically Christians have been divided as to how exactly the Bible regulates worship. Some are of the opinion that we may do anything in worship except what the Bible explicitly prohibits, while others insist that we may do only what the Bible explicitly commands. Presbyterians have tended to opt for the second position. Allowing it to regulate our worship is not restrictive, because of the wide range of activities the Bible tells us ought to go on in worship. Here are some things that the Bible says should take place when the church meets to reach up to God in worship.

➢ Greetings and benedictions. They were a regular feature of Paul's letters (Romans 1:7 1 Corinthians 1:3 and 16:23-24 and 2 and 15:33, 2 Corinthians 13:14), and since these letters were most likely read at church meetings, these greetings and benedictions were part of worship.

➢ The reading of the Bible. In the Jewish synagogue, the Old Testament was read (Luke 4:17-19 and Acts 15:21), and the first Christians carried on this practice (1 Timothy 4:13).

➢ The preaching of the Bible. God wants His Word to be taught, as well as read, in services of worship (2 Timothy 4:2).

➢ Prayer. It goes without saying that prayer is a legitimate component of worship, with our services sprinkled with prayers of adoration, thanksgiving, confession and petition (Philippians 4:4-6 and 1 Timothy 2:1).

➢ Singing. Songs are means by which we express our thanks to God, our sorrow over sin, our commitment to Jesus and by which we learn more about God and His ways (Ephesians 5:19-20, Colossians 3:16 and 1 Chronicles 16:9).

➢ The celebration of God's salvation in the sacraments of baptism and the Lord's Supper (Acts 2:42 and 46).

➢ Collections and offerings. Paul tells the church in Corinth to collect money when they meet together to worship (1 Corinthians 16:1-2), and he informs the Christians at Philippi that the giving of gifts is an act of worship (Philippians 4:18).

➢ Participation. Whatever our understanding of the gifts of tongues, interpretation of tongues and prophecy, it is clear from what Paul said in 1 Corinthians 14 that, while a

151

service must not be an uncontrollable free-for-all (1 Corinthians 14:33 and 40), more than one person should take part in the service (1 Corinthians 14:26-32).

➤ To this list could be added the making of vows to God (Psalm 50:14 and Psalm 65:1), declarations of what we believe (Philippians 2:6-11 and 1 Timothy 3:16), and expressions of fellowship (Romans 16:16).

If all this sounds suspiciously like a defence of a classic worship service, then in some ways it is. The reason why we do what we do in a classic worship service is not due to the fact that we are stuck in a time warp, or because we are not very creative in our thinking and so find it impossible to be innovative in worship. We do what we do because we only want to follow the Bible's instructions. To move beyond what the Bible says and to introduce what it does not command into our worship would be dishonour God, and that is the last thing we want to do.

Worship is to be **personality-engaging**. We worship God in the totality of our personalities, so in our services our minds must be engaged, our emotions stirred and our wills moved. Services that simply try to hype people up emotionally and are all touchy-feely without attempting to get them to think, or that have no warmth in them because they are directed only at people's minds, or that do not make an effort to challenge people to think, feel and live differently are sub-standard.

Worship is to be **culturally-relevant**. If we are to praise God, pray to Him and listen to His Word with understanding (1 Corinthians 14:15 and Ephesians 5:17), then the bottom line is that our services must be conducted in language with which we are familiar.

Worship is to be **love-driven**. Sometimes we are guilty of giving the impression that worship is a chore. How can worship be a chore when we think of who God is and what He has done for us in Jesus? Our Spirit-generated love for Jesus will make us

152

anticipate worship with the same sense of excitement that a couple approach their first date.

Worship is to be **life-impacting**. The way in which some Christians use the term as a synonym for praise downgrades worship. Churches employ worship leaders, whose main task is to lead the congregational singing, and churches advertise their services as a time of "worship and the Word". Another way in which we are guilty of dumming down worship is by restricting it to what goes on for an hour or so on a Sunday morning. A minister friend of mine has this written on the back of his church's notice board: "The service is over, but the worship isn't". He wants to remind everyone that worship is something we do every day of the week, and it is not a Sunday-morning-only activity. If what we do on a Sunday morning makes no difference to the way we live from Monday to Saturday, it is below par worship.

> In most congregations it is the minister who plans and leads worship, though in some the elders or a worship team assists him. If worship is to be all that we have just considered, then we ought to be constantly praying for these people. It is not an easy thing to prepare and deliver quality services of worship week after week. These people should be the objects of our prayers, and not the butt of our criticism.

❖ THE CHURCH REACHES OUT TO OTHERS IN MISSION

In a popular quiz show, a contestant was asked if the saying "Charity begins at home" was found in the Bible. Guess what he answered? Right first time! Sadly he is not alone in thinking that this saying is found in the Bible. Some Christians think it is and many act as if it is. They almost view the church as their private club, with little or no interest in what goes on beyond the front door of the church building. Jesus is constantly challenging our narrow-mindedness and telling us to reach out to those outside the church in mission (Luke 10:2, John 4:35 and Acts 1:6-8).

What does the church's mission involve? Towards the end of each of the Gospels and at the start of Acts, you come across some of Jesus' final instructions to the church (Matthew 28:18-20, Mark 16:15, Luke 24:46-47, John 20:21 and Acts 1:8). Those statements indicate that the church's mission involves evangelism and social action. The church is to announce the message that Jesus, the Son of God, entered this world as a real human being to die as a substitute for sinners. God raised Him from the dead to validate His claims and endorse His achievements (Romans 1:3-4). The church is then to uncompromisingly present God's demand that people turn from their sins, trust in Jesus as Saviour and follow Him as Lord (Acts 20:21 and Romans 1:5), and finally to assure people that, if they do what God wants them to do, He has promised to pardon their sins (Acts 10:43). Running parallel to the church's proclamation of the good news, and complementing it, the church is to be at the cutting edge of social action. We are not only to preach grace; we are also to do justice. The reason for this is that our mission is modelled on Jesus (John 20:21), and, as He came into the world to serve those in need, so the church is to serve human need wherever we encounter it (Luke 10:30-37). Jesus' command to take the good news to all the world (Mark 16:15) does not supersede or exhaust Jesus' command to love our neighbours in the same way as we love ourselves (Mark 12:31).

Where does the church's mission take place? Mission is to be done where the people with spiritual, physical and emotional needs are. Just as Jesus was sent into the world to carry out His mission, so we are sent into the world to fulfil our mission (John 17:18). Sadly we have turned the model Jesus gives us on its head, expecting people to come to our patch rather than going out and engaging with people on their own turf.

Acts 1:8 informs us of where the church's mission is to take place.

➤ In Jerusalem – in familiar territory such as our homes and wider family circle.

154

> In Judea – among people who are of the same culture as us, such as our friends, work colleagues and the people with whom we study and play sport.
> In Samaria – among people who live close at hand but who are of a different religious, cultural and political background from us.
> In all the world – going cross-cultural and international with Jesus' mission.

Who takes part in the church's mission? Even a surface reading of the book of Acts would throw up the conclusion that every Christian took part in the church's mission. This is particularly clear in what happened to the Jerusalem Church after Stephen was martyred. As the Jewish religious authorities began to clamp down on the church, the church leaders remained in Jerusalem while the ordinary Christians were forced out of town. These ordinary Christians began to take the good news to wherever they went (Acts 8:1-4). Clearly participation in the church's mission is not restricted to a small elite group of Christians; it is the responsibility of every Christian. Jesus' instructions for mission rest upon the whole church collectively, and therefore upon each Christian individually.

Why should Christians be part of the church's mission? The Bible gives three motives for mission, and the first one is obedience to Jesus' commands. His commands are clear, so, if we are not involved in mission, we are openly disobeying Jesus. Another motive is love and compassion for those in need (2 Corinthians 5:14). The highest motive for mission is a deep-seated longing to see Jesus given His proper place in people's lives. Jesus is Lord, but so many people in our world give their loyalty and allegiance to substitute gods, worshipping their career, their family, their political cause, their sport, their education and ultimately themselves rather than worshipping Jesus. When we see that happening, we should be distressed and want to go to them and plead with them to let go of their idols and start putting Jesus first in their lives. It was this burning passion to see Jesus given His proper place in people's lives that motivated Paul in his mission to Athens (Acts 17:16-17).

❖ THE CHURCH REACHES IN TO EACH OTHER IN FELLOWSHIP

Although the church is concerned about its non-members, like any functional family, it tries to look after its own. The word "fellowship" is another biblical idea that has been downgraded in the contemporary church. It means much more than people having a cup of coffee and a chat after the service instead of rushing off home. What the word "fellowship" looks like can be seen from the "one another" and the "each other" statements scattered throughout the New Testament. First and foremost, God calls on us to love each other (Romans 13:8; 1 Thessalonians 4:9; 1 Peter 1:22 and 4:8; 1 John 3:11, 3:22, 4:7, 4:11 and 4:12; and 2 John 1:5), but how do we do that? Once again God has not left us to guess because, just as His Word regulates our worship of Him, so it also controls our relationship with our fellow Christians. We are to be devoted to one another (Romans 12:10), live in harmony with each other (Romans 12:16), and accept one another (Romans 15:7). We are to serve one another (Galatians 5:13) and carry each other's burdens (Galatians 6:2). When someone rubs us up the wrong way, we are to be patient with them (Ephesians 4:2), and when they do or say something to hurt us, we are to forgive them as God has forgiven us (Ephesians 4:32). We are to teach one another (Colossians 3:16). Instead of putting other Christians down, we are to pray for them (James 5:16) and encourage them (1 Thessalonians 5:11). Rather than provoking other Christians by our irritating habits, we are to spur them on in their pursuit of godliness (Hebrews 10:24). We are to show our love for other Christians by greeting them when we bump into them in the street (Romans 16:16), by having them in our homes for meals (1 Peter 4:9), and by refusing to run them down in front of our children and those who are not Christians (James 5:9).

However, fellowship also has a very practical side to it as we look after each others material needs. This was certainly true of the Jerusalem Church (Acts 2:44 and Acts 4:32 and 34-35), and it ought to be a feature of our congregational life.

The nosedive in church attendance, especially in urban areas but increasingly in rural areas too, signals the fact that many in our society regard the church as an irrelevancy. Rather than getting sucked into that way of thinking about it, we need to recapture the biblical perspective about the key role the church plays in our Christian lives. Our "primary purpose is to glorify God and to enjoy Him" (*The Shorter Catechism* Question 1), and while certainly wanting to encourage private Bible reading, prayer and singing, God's presence is also enjoyed when Christians meet together to worship Him (Psalm 149:1-2 and Matthew 18:20). Jesus' final instructions to us focused on taking the good news to the whole world (Acts 1:8), and this is most effectively done as Christians work together. The defining characteristic of the Christian is love for other Christians (John 13:35), and love is not a quality we display on our own because to love, we need at least one more person. We cannot properly do what we are supposed to do as Christians in isolation, so when people ask "Who needs the church?", our immediate reply should be "I do".

DIGGING DEEPER

You might like to explore further some of the issues raised in this chapter by reading *The Church* by Edmund Clowney (Published by IVP) and *Understanding the Church* by David Jackman (Published by Christian Focus Publications).

12. PICTURES AND PROMISES

In this chapter we are going to discover what the Bible says about baptism and the Lord's Supper.
- The sacraments are authorised by Jesus
- The sacraments are intended to make our faith in Jesus stronger
- The sacraments are pictures of God's salvation
- The sacraments are promises of God's salvation

BAPTISM
- The what of baptism

An indication of admission to the visible church
A sign of what God's salvation is like
A seal of God's covenant promise
- The who of baptism

Christians who have not been previously baptised, and believers' children
- The how of baptism

Immersion as the only way to baptise is not proven
Pouring / sprinkling is the preferable way to administer baptism

THE LORD'S SUPPER
- We look back to the cross with gratitude
- We look up to Jesus with a renewed sense of commitment to Him
- We look into our hearts with self-examination
- We look around to other Christians in love
- We look out to the world in witness
- We look forward to heaven with anticipation

Several years ago, a colleague, who was not known for being on the cutting edge of technological innovation (some of us suspected that he used a quill to write his sermons), surprised his family and friends by buying a computer. In an attempt to combat his almost total computer illiteracy, he enrolled in an evening class with the promising title "A basic introduction to your computer". However, he almost did not finish the course, and what he found most off-putting was not the way the course tutor constantly used jargon, but that he did not bother to explain what the terms meant.

I have had to use some jargon in my outline of the main themes of the Bible – it is almost impossible to avoid doing so – but I tried hard not to make that course tutor's mistake and attempted to explain the meaning of the various theological terms I have used. Without wanting to stretch your patience to breaking point, I have one more technical term that I want to throw in your direction; it is the word "sacrament".

Let me try to build up a profile of the Bible's understanding of this term.

❖ **AUTHORISED BY JESUS**

For something to be regarded as a sacrament it had be sanctioned by Jesus as one. This means that only baptism and the Lord's Supper can be legitimately labelled "sacraments" because they were the only ones authorised by Jesus. On the night before His death, Jesus inaugurated the sacrament of the Lord's Supper (Matthew 26:26-28, Mark 14:22-24, Luke 22:19-20 and 1 Corinthians 11:23-26), and, as part of His final instructions to His followers, He established the sacrament of baptism (Matthew 28:18-20). "Sacraments" is a collective term that refers exclusively to baptism and the Lord's Supper.

❖ **INTENDED TO MAKE OUR FAITH IN JESUS STRONGER**

In bringing us to faith in Jesus, the Holy Spirit does not use the sacraments but the Bible (2 Timothy 3:15 and 1 Peter 1:23). However, to strengthen our faith in Jesus, the Holy Spirit not only uses the Bible, but also the sacraments. In his overall strategy, God's intention is that baptism and the Lord's Supper consolidate a faith in Jesus that is already there.

In our attitude towards the sacraments we need balance,

neither playing down nor playing up their importance. On the one hand, if Jesus authorised the sacraments to make our faith in Him stronger, then it is spiritually detrimental to be consistently absent from services during which baptism is administered and the Lord's Supper celebrated. On the other hand it is possible to attach to the sacraments an importance the Bible does not give to them. There will be people in heaven who have neither been baptised nor been at the Lord's Supper, because the outward physical act of having water poured on you or of eating a piece of bread and drinking a little wine does not, in itself, bring about an inward spiritual change in us.

❖ PICTURES OF GOD'S SALVATION

In His desire to help us understand what He has done for us, God not only appeals to our sense of hearing by telling us in the Bible what His salvation is like, He also appeals to our sense of sight by illustrating it in the sacraments. In fact, in the Lord's Supper, He appeals to our sense of taste, touch and smell as well. Imagine that you are driving along a road that you have never been on before in your life. As you approach a bend, you see a sign, which warns you about a junction just around the corner. You cannot see the junction, but the sign informs you that it is there. The sacraments function like that road sign; they depict something unseen. In them, God uses water (in baptism) and bread and wine (in the Lord's Supper), which are outward, physical and visible, to give a picture of inward, spiritual and invisible realities. What these actually are, we will see when we look at them separately. Baptism and the Lord's Supper are visual aids that point away from themselves to God's salvation.

❖ PROMISES OF GOD'S SALVATION

We all suspected that, in spite of the macho image he liked to project, Harry was a big softie at heart. We were right, because he proposed to Carly, his girlfriend, down on one knee with a red rose in his hand after dinner on Valentine's Day. Carly accepted, and the next day she appeared proudly wearing an engagement ring. That engagement ring was visual confirmation that they had made promises to each other that one day they would get married. God has promised us salvation. His Word ought to be enough, but because our faith is weak and we doubt His Word, God has given us the sacraments as a visual confirmation of the promises He has made. Just as the rainbow visually reassured Noah of the trustworthiness of God's promise never again to destroy the world by means of a flood (Genesis 9:12-16), so baptism and the Lord's Supper visually reassure us of God's promise to save us.

As we understand the function of the sacraments as pictures and promises of God's salvation – theologians usually use the phrase "signs and seals of the Covenant of Grace" – so our faith in Jesus is strengthened.

➢ One of the reasons why our faith becomes weak is that we forget what God has done for us (Psalm 78:11 and Psalm 106:7, 13 and 21). To counteract this cause of spiritual decline, we are to continually remember what God has done for us (Psalm 103:2 and Psalm 105:5). The recollection of God's salvation motivates us to live for Jesus with a renewed energy and enthusiasm (Romans 12:1). God has given us the sacraments to help us remember what He has done, because, as we look beyond the outward and physical elements to the inward and spiritual realities they signify, we recall God's salvation, and so our faith is strengthened.

➢ An indication that something is not right with our spiritual health is a lack of assurance of salvation. We usually imagine that the way to deal with this spiritual problem is to look for some stunning spiritual encounter with God in which we will almost audibly hear Him tell us that He still loves us. This spectacular experience seldom materialises, because God's normal means of bringing assurance is quite unglamorous. He reassures us of His love in the Bible's promises and then visually confirms them to us in baptism and the Lord's Supper. It is through the unspectacular means of the Word and the sacraments that we come to realise that we continue to be on the receiving end of God's love. We see this in Abraham's spiritual journey. In Genesis 15, God promised Abraham salvation, and, when Abraham took God at His word, he discovered himself in a right relationship with God (Genesis 15:1-6). As confirmation of His promise to him, God appeared to Abraham in one of the most spectacular displays of His glory in the Old Testament (Genesis 15:8-20). However, in Genesis 16, we come across the ugly incident involving Abraham and Hagar. With his faith at an all-time low, Abraham probably wondered if he had blown it as far as God was concerned. Then, in Genesis 17, God repeated His promises of salvation to Abraham. God wanted to give Abraham something that would reassure him that his sin had not disqualified him from receiving His promises. This time instead of having a spectacular spiritual experience, he received the sign of circumcision, and by it God visually confirmed to Abraham His spoken promise (Genesis 17:1-2) that he was still the recipient of His promises of salvation (Romans 4:11). It was a combination of Word and sacrament (for circumcision was the Old Testament counterpart of baptism) that brought Abraham peace of mind about his relationship with God, and God normally uses the same combination, not stunning spiritual encounters with Him, to bring assurance to our hearts.

BAPTISM

The discussion was generating more heat than light, with voices becoming gradually more raised as opinions were increasingly stated more stridently. Tempers were becoming frayed. This was not a group of politicians squabbling over an emotive issue such as whether or not the United Kingdom should join the Euro Zone. It was a group of Christian students arguing about baptism. A few hours earlier they had been worshipping together at the Christian Union meeting, but now they were almost coming to blows. Tragically, Christians are deeply divided about baptism, and the controversy rages over three matters – the meaning, subjects and mode of baptism.

❖ THE WHAT OF BAPTISM

An indication of admission to the visible church In the Old Testament, the mark of admission into the visible church, those with whom God had entered into covenant, was circumcision (Genesis 17:14), and God warned that any male who was not circumcised was not part of the fellowship of God's people (Genesis 17:14). Baptism has now replaced circumcision as the indicator of those who are members of the visible church, the community related to God by covenant (Acts 2:41, Acts 10:44-48, Galatians 3:27-29).

> Some churches divorce baptism and admission into the visible church as they are prepared to baptise people without incorporating them into their congregations. It is essential that those who are baptised are part of a congregation, because it is within the context of the visible church, with its preaching, administration of the sacraments and opportunities for service, that the Christian's faith develops.

A sign of what God's salvation is like Throughout the Bible, circumcision is presented as a sign pointing to what the promises God makes in the Covenant of Grace are like (Genesis 17:11 and Romans 4:11). Baptism has now replaced circumcision as the sign of the covenant (Colossians 2:11-12), so it too functions like a signpost, directing our attention away from itself to what God's salvation is like. In the Bible, the symbol of washing with water and the idea of baptism are linked with cleansing from sin (Ezekiel 36:25), forgiveness of sins (Acts 2:38), union with Jesus (Romans 6:23), adoption into God's family (Galatians 3:26-27), the new birth (John 3:3 and 5), the gift of the Holy Spirit (Ezekiel 36:25-27) and the resurrection to eternal life (Romans 6:5). Baptism's function is to tell us what God does when He saves a person.

This is one of the places where Presbyterians and Baptists part company. Baptists see baptism as a sign of the baptised person's faith, but that is not how the Bible sees baptism. Baptism in the Bible is not a sign of human faith, pointing to what we have done, but it is a sign of God's grace, pointing to what He has done. One of the most common objections to the Presbyterian position on baptism is that infants are too young to turn from their sin to trust in Jesus. This criticism should not faze us at all because it is based on the false assumption that baptism is a sign of human faith. It is a sign of God's salvation, so it is does not really matter if the infant who is baptised is young. What is being announced in a baptism is not what the baptised person has done, but what God has done.

A seal of God's covenant promise Circumcision was not only a sign of the Covenant of Grace, but also a seal of the covenant (Romans 4:11); not just a picture, but also a promise. The same is true of baptism. Our baptism reminds us that God has promised to actively work in our lives to make all His covenant promises real in our experience. Sometimes as Christians we fail God so badly we begin to believe Satan's spin that God wants nothing more to do with us. Our baptism knocks the devil's innuendo on the head as it is God's guarantee to us that He will never let us go. It is a promise of God's commitment to bring us into and keep us in a right relationship with Himself until we safely arrive in heaven (Philippians 1:6). When we stupidly go our own way, He disciplines us to bring us back into line, but even that discipline is a sign of His unwavering love and firm commitment to us (Hebrews 12:6).

❖ THE WHO OF BAPTISM

I was once invited to speak to a group of young adults about baptism, and began by asking them whom do Presbyterians believed should be baptised. "Easy," one of them immediately replied, "Presbyterians believe in baptising babies". That is not exactly what Presbyterians believe the Bible teaches about who should be baptised. The Bible does not give us to the go-ahead to baptise every single baby, but only the children of Christians. In addition, and this may come as a surprise to some, it also authorises us to baptise adults who have become Christians but who have not been previously baptised.

The reason why we baptise *both* categories of people is because of what the Bible says about the Covenant of Grace in general and God's covenant with Abraham in particular. Several relevant facts emerge from Genesis 17:1-14. God took the initiative and established His covenant with Abraham (Genesis 17:7), and when God entered into covenant with Abraham, he was a believer who was in a right relationship with God because he trusted in Jesus (Genesis 15:6 and Romans 4:1-12). However, God not only entered into covenant with Abraham, He also made His covenant with Abraham's descendants (Genesis 17:7). What was the spiritual status of Abraham's descendants? They were the children of a believer. How did Abraham and his descendants know that God had entered into covenant with them? God gave them the sign of circumcision (Genesis 17:10-11). So the believer, who had not been previously circumcised, and the believer's children were to be circumcised to show that God entered into covenant with them.

What has all this got to do with baptism? God's covenant is described as "an everlasting covenant" (Genesis 17:7), which means that the covenant arrangements God established with Abraham are still operative today. He promises the same salvation to us as He promised to Abraham, and on the same basis – faith in Jesus. Just as in Abraham's time, God makes these promises to the believer and the believer's children. Also, and this is where the relevance of the covenant to baptism kicks in, the sign of the covenant is to be administered to the same categories of people as it was in Abraham's time – the believer and the believer's children. The only change between now and Abraham's time is that, in keeping with the fact that the new administration of the covenant is broader in its application than the old administration, baptism has replaced circumcision as the covenant sign so that females, as well as males, can receive it. It is only within the framework of the Bible's teaching about the Covenant of Grace that we find the biblical sanction for baptising *both* adults who have become Christians but who have not been previously baptised *and* the children of Christians.

In addition to the argument based on the Bible's teaching on the Covenant of Grace, Presbyterians present other Bible-based reasons for baptising the children of Christians.

➢ If members of the visible church have the right to participate in the sacraments and if baptism is a sacrament and believers' children are part of the visible church, then they have the right to be baptised.

➢ Baptism is an entitlement of all who belong to God's Kingdom, and Jesus makes it clear that believers' children are members of God's Kingdom (Luke 18:16).

➢ Baptists claim that there are no examples of infants being baptised in the New Testament, but that is not necessarily the case. In the New Testament there are three examples of household baptism (Acts 16:15, Acts 16:33 and 1 Corinthians 1:15), and while admitting that the Bible does not explicitly say that any of these three family

166

groups contained children, it does not say that they did not. Although it does not prove conclusively that the first Christians baptised believers' children, the household baptisms do give grounds to question the claim that there are no examples of infants being baptised in the New Testament.

➤ Andrew picked up the Bible on top of the coffee table, held it up, and, turning to me, asked, "Rodger, show me a single verse in the New Testament which clearly states believers' children are to be baptised". I couldn't, because there aren't as the New Testament is silent about the matter. However, far from demolishing the Presbyterian position on who should be baptised, the New Testament's silence actually supports it. Why does the New Testament not bother to mention this matter? Simply because the baptism of believers' children was taken as read, so there was no need to specifically mention it. Baptising believers' children was so much the norm that it was never challenged, and so the New Testament writers never had a reason to raise the matter. This argument from the New Testament's silence is not to be sniffed at as we use it to sanction other things we do. For example, there is not a single statement in the New Testament that clearly states that women should take part in the Lord's Supper, but the thought has never entered our head to ban women from the Lord's Supper. Besides, the argument from silence cuts both ways. Just as there is no single New Testament verse which clearly states that believers' children were baptised, so there is no single New Testament verse which clearly mentions the baptism as adults of children whose parents were Christians and who were brought up in a Christian home. We have to graciously point out to our Baptist

friends that they cannot have it both ways.

❖ **THE HOW OF BAPTISM**

Baptists are insistent that there is only one way to administer baptism, and that is by being totally immersed in water. Their case for immersion rests upon three claims: the Greek verbs *bapto* and *baptizo*, from which we obviously get our English word "baptism", always mean to immerse; the New Testament's description of some baptisms implies immersion; and what baptism symbolises can only be represented by immersion. However, the Baptist case for immersion is not as watertight as they would like to make out.

The Greek verbs *bapto* and *baptizo* do not always mean to immerse. There are places where they might (Leviticus 11:32 and Job 9:31), but there are also places were it is highly questionable that they do (Leviticus 14:6 and 51, Ruth 2:14, 1 Samuel 14:27, Daniel 4:30, Daniel 5:21, Luke 11:38 and 1 Corinthians 10:3).

Baptists suggest that, when Matthew and Mark write about Jesus coming up out of the water at His baptism (Matthew 3:16 and Mark 1:10), they are implying that Jesus first went down under the water and then came up from under it. That is simply reading far too much into what Matthew and Mark are saying.

Baptists point to Romans 6:3-4 as indisputable proof that the symbolism of baptism – being united to Jesus in His death and resurrection – can only be represented by being immersed in water in order to emerge from it. However, in Romans 6, Paul describes the Christian's union with Jesus, not just in terms of being buried with Him (Romans 6:4), but also in terms of being planted with Him (Romans 6:5) and being crucified with Him (Romans 6:6). These last two expressions represent our union with Jesus as much as being buried with Him, but there is no way that they can be represented by immersion. What Baptists do in running with only one of the pictures Paul gives in Romans 6 for our union with Jesus and basing their insistence that baptism must be by immersion on it, while ignoring the other two Romans 6 pictures for our union with Jesus is a bit dodgy.

In the Scottish legal system, three verdicts can be given: guilty, not guilty, and not proven. The Baptist case for baptism exclusively by immersion is, at best, not proven.

Presbyterians hold that the Bible teaches that pouring or sprinkling is a valid way to baptise people. Our position is based on the following lines of biblical thought.

Throughout the Bible there is a clear connection between the salvation offered in the Covenant of Grace and the mode of sprinkling (Exodus 24:5-8, Isaiah 52:13-53:12 and especially Isaiah 53:15, Ezekiel 36:25-28, Hebrews 12:24 and 1 Peter 1:2).

The way baptism is administered must correspond to its meaning. Surely the best means of representing the Holy Spirit falling upon us, to bring union with Jesus and cleansing from sin, is as water falls on us from above.

The first Christians baptised by pouring / sprinkling. Central to their understanding of baptism was the idea of cleansing from sin. On three occasions the Old Testament links cleansing with bathing (Leviticus 14:8, Leviticus 15:13 and Numbers 19:19), and this might hint at immersion. However, in the majority of instances, the Old Testament links cleansing with sprinkling. It would be perfectly natural to assume that, when they administered a sacrament that symbolised cleansing, the first Christians, who were Jews, would fall back on their Jewish heritage and use the same mode associated with cleansing in the Old Testament – sprinkling.

John the Baptist baptised by pouring / sprinkling, and not by immersion. John predicted that his baptism with water pointed forward to a baptism of the Holy Spirit to be carried out by Jesus (Matthew 3:11, Mark 1:8, Luke 3:16 and John 1:33). John's prophecy was fulfilled on the Day of Pentecost, and the baptism by the Spirit, which took place that day, cannot be conceived of as an immersion. In fact, in Acts 2:17, it is specifically described as a pouring out. If the baptism by the Spirit was by pouring, then John's baptism, which pointed to it, would also have to be administered by pouring.

Jesus was baptised by pouring / sprinkling because He was

baptised by John (Matthew 3:13 and Mark 1:9). Also, when He preached in His hometown synagogue, Jesus applied Isaiah 61:1-2 to Himself, claiming that He was anointed by the Holy Spirit for His Messianic work of being God's prophet, priest and king (Luke 4:16-21). This anointing took place when He was baptised, and the mode that best symbolises Jesus' anointing with the Holy Spirit is pouring / sprinkling. Jesus saw His baptism as His ordination to the priesthood for when the Jewish religious authorities challenged Him about the way He had cleansed the Temple (Luke 19:45-46 and Luke 20:1-2), something only a priest could do, Jesus referred them back to His baptism by John (Luke 20:3-4). Jesus is saying that He has every right to act as a priest and purify the Temple from defilement because He had been ordained as a priest when John baptised Him. For a priest's ordination to be valid, he had to be thirty years old (Numbers 4:3 and 47), and Jesus was thirty when He was baptised (Luke 3:23). Then, a priest had to be called by God (Exodus 28:1), and this was also true of Jesus (Hebrews 5:4-10). Also a priest had to be ordained by someone who was a priest (Exodus 29:9 and Numbers 25:13), and Jesus' baptism was performed by John, who, as well as undoubtedly being a prophet, had also priestly credentials as he came from a priestly family (Luke 1:5). Finally, and most significant of all, in order to be properly ordained, a priest had to be sprinkled with water (Numbers 8:6-7). As Jesus' baptism was a valid ordination to the priesthood, John did not immerse Jesus in the River Jordan; he poured / sprinkled water on Him.

The weight of the Bible's evidence seems to be pointing away from immersion towards pouring / sprinkling as the preferable way to administer baptism.

We need to hold our views on baptism firmly and with conviction because we believe that they reflect the Bible's teaching about the matter. However, we need to hold them in love and with understanding towards those who will disagree with us. Different views on baptism must never be allowed to become a barrier to fellowship between Christians. The basis of our fellowship is not that we think the same way about baptism and how and to whom it should be administered. It is that our great covenant-making and covenant-keeping God sent His one and only Son to die for us, and, by the gracious activity of His Holy Spirit in our lives, brought us to faith in Jesus and adopted us into His family, so that we are now sisters and brothers in Jesus.

THE LORD'S SUPPER

Imagine that someone who has never been to church in her life turns up at your church. She sits beside you and bombards you with questions about what is happening and why it is happening and what it means. It is a Communion Sunday, and she is really fascinated by what she sees happening. So she asks you to explain to her what is going on. What would you say to her? Here are six statements you could use to explain to her the various shades of meaning attached to the Lord's Supper.

❖ WE LOOK BACK TO THE CROSS WITH GRATITUDE

This is the most obvious meaning of the Lord's Supper for twice Jesus said, "Do this in remembrance of Me" (1 Corinthians 11:24 and 25). Jesus wanted the Lord's Supper to take His followers back to His death on the cross as the broken bread depicted His body that would be broken in death (1 Corinthians 11:24), and the poured out wine pointed to His blood that would be spilt in death (1 Corinthians 11:24). The primary objective of the Lord's Supper is to get us to look back to the day when Jesus died on the Hill of the Skull in order to remember all the blessings that came our way as a result of His death.

Remembering Jesus' death should not be something cold and formal. We should be filled with a profound sense of gratitude because we recognise that Jesus died so that our sins could be dealt with effectively. As we see the bread being broken and the wine being poured out, take them in our hands, place them in our mouths and swallow them, we should say to ourselves, "Jesus' body was broken in death *for me*, and His blood was shed in death *for me*", and this should fill our hearts with thankfulness. The Lord's Supper is not a sad occasion, but a time for Spirit-generated joy in what our Saviour has done for us (Psalm 116:12-13).

❖ WE LOOK UP TO JESUS WITH A RENEWED SENSE OF COMMITMENT TO HIM

Jesus is present with us as we celebrate the Lord's Supper, not in a literal physical way because His resurrected body is in heaven (Hebrews 1:3) but in a spiritual way through the activity of the Holy Spirit. Jesus is at the Lord's Supper not to be seen or touched but to be received by faith. Jesus' presence at the Lord's Supper is genuine as He is personally present through His Spirit.

Nearly everyone who writes about the sacraments points out that the word "sacrament" is not found in the Bible but comes from the Latin word "sacramentum", which was an oath of loyalty that a Roman soldier swore to his commanding officer. While that may be true, the idea of taking part in the sacraments committing us to Jesus is biblical. As we recognise that Jesus is really there at the Lord's Supper and look up to Him as our Saviour and Lord, we will not just want to express our gratitude to Him for what He has done in praise and thanksgiving, we will want to commit ourselves to Him in a fresh way (Psalm 116:12-14).

❖ WE LOOK INTO OUR HEARTS WITH SELF EXAMINATION

The Lord's Supper is often given the term "Communion" (1 Corinthians 10:16 in the King James Version). The word means "to have fellowship", and reminds us that, at the Lord's Supper, we have fellowship with Jesus. A practical implication of this is that we should take a look into our hearts to see if there is any sin there, which will short-circuit our fellowship with Jesus. This is why Paul instructs us to do some self-examination before we come to the Lord's Supper (1 Corinthians 11:28). In a sane and balanced way we are to ask if our faith in Jesus is still strong, if our desire to turn away from sin is still real, if our love for Jesus is still warm, and if our obedience to Jesus is still wholehearted and motivated by love for Him.

❖ WE LOOK AROUND TO OTHER CHRISTIANS IN LOVE

Jesus is not the only person with whom we commune at the Lord's Supper; we also have fellowship with other Christians. The Lord's Supper is not a self-served meal that we enjoy alone. We eat and drink with other members of the church. It expresses the unity of the congregation as we all eat the same bread (1 Corinthians 10:17) and drink from the same cup, we all sit around the same table, and we all eat and drink together. This means that we must not be guilty of doing anything that might ruin our fellowship with one another. If we have done anything that has caused a break-up in the congregation's unity, we are to take steps to sort that problem out before we come to the Lord's Supper (Matthew 5:23-24).

Sylvia was a Christian, but she never took part in the Lord's Supper. When Robert, her minister, asked her why, she told him it was Paul's warning not to come to the Lord's Supper "in an unworthy manner" (1 Corinthians 11:27) that kept her away. She felt unworthy and believed that her sense of unworthiness disqualified her from coming to the Lord's Supper. Robert pointed out to her that no one was worthy to come, and that Christians were often overwhelmed with feelings of unworthiness as they remembered Jesus' love in dying for them, but Paul was not talking about that. He was speaking about the way in which people came to the Lord's Supper. Gently he explained to Sylvia that coming "in an unworthy manner" meant insisting in taking part in the Lord's Supper in spite of not being prepared to admit and turn away from the coldness, hardness and carelessness

that has crept into our relationship with Jesus and not
being prepared to admit and turn away from the bitterness,
resentment and selfishness that has contaminated our lives
and which ruins our relationship with other Christians.
Several weeks later, when the church met to remember the
Jesus' death, Sylvia was there, and as they prepared to eat
the bread and drink the wine Charles Wesley's great hymn
Jesus, lover of my soul was sung. As they sang the lines
"Just and holy is Your name,
I am all unworthiness;
false and full of sin I am,
You are full of truth and grace",
Sylvia was not the only one with tears in her eyes.

❖ WE LOOK OUT TO THE WORLD IN WITNESS

In word and action the Lord's Supper broadcasts the good
news (1 Corinthians 11:26). The bread and the wine tell people
about Jesus' death, but the Lord's Supper also calls on people to
personally trust Jesus. Jesus did not just break bread and pour out
wine; He also gave it to His followers to eat and drink. He not
only said, "This is My body" and "This is My blood", He also
said, "Take and eat" and "Drink from [this cup], all of you"
(Matthew 26:26-27). Jesus does not simply want people to
remember His death; He also wants them to share in the benefits
of His death. So He not only carries out symbolic actions, which
point to His death, He also invites His followers to share a meal.
Our witness to the world is not just the announcements of facts
about who Jesus is and what He did; it is also an invitation to
people to trust in Him.

❖ WE LOOK FORWARD TO HEAVEN WITH ANTICIPATION

Just as the Passover was temporary, so the Lord's Supper is
also confined to time (1 Corinthians 11:26). One day, Jesus will
return and gather His people together in heaven for "the

Marriage Supper of the Lamb" (Revelation 19:9). Each Lord's Supper should remind us of our hope as Christians and fill our hearts with a longing for Jesus to return.

DIGGING DEEPER

You might like to explore further some of the issues raised in ethis chapter by reading *Salvation's Sign and Seal: The case for infant baptism* by Rodger M Crooks (Published by Christian Focus Publications), *The Lord's Supper* by Gordon Keddie (Published by Evangelical Press), and *Remembering Jesus* by Steve Motyer (Published by Christian Focus Publications).